GIVING
WISELY?

Praise for *Giving Wisely?*

Jonathan Martin's book *Giving Wisely?* is a significant contribution to the body of Christ, raising important questions that demand good answers. We need to give more generously and more strategically at the same time, being careful not to harm the very people we want to help. As a former missionary and now missions pastor at my home church, I have seen Jonathan bring rich experience and passion to this subject. He offers guidelines that alert and encourage us toward giving that will have a lasting impact. I commend Jonathan for his transparency about his own growth in this area, and his heart to encourage individuals and organizations to give more, but at the same time give more wisely.

Randy Alcorn
Author of *The Treasure Principle* and *Money, Possessions & Eternity*

Jonathan Martin is trustworthy. His great heart, his creative mind, and his bright spirit are contagious. His wisdom in the world of global missions comes first hand. Twelve years among Communists and Muslims in closed regions with his young family provide a foundational experience for his current role as Pastor of Global and Community Outreach at Good Shepherd Church. Our Lord is using Jonathan to rejuvenate this church's outreach both here and in the farthest corner. The RAISE principles in this book are near the heart of that vibrancy. Devour it.

Stu Weber
Author of *Tender Warrior* and *Infinite Impact*

This is an incredible, 'Must Read' book by all those who care and give to missions and charitable concerns. Jonathan brings unusual, practical wisdom and experience to bear on how we give and support causes overseas as well as locally. He and his family have lived and worked in the field and have seen first hand what happens on the other side of the fence when we "throw" our money at good causes in bad ways.

Lew Feucht
Chief Quality Officer
Fortune 500 High Tech Firm

Anyone going anywhere cross-culturally for any reason should read this book. Using the Bible, personal stories, and a heart of instruction, Jonathan gives a refresher course on God's plan for generous giving, but with a twist - how to be generous where all the rules are different than our own. After helping to send thousands of short-term workers to over eighty countries, I have seen first hand the shocking effects of misappropriated giving. I've also seen the extraordinary blessings of appropriate generosity. "Giving Wisely?" takes the guess work out of generous giving to other cultures. This should be required reading for every short-term ministry leader!

Brian Heerwagen
Author of *The Next Mile*
Executive Director, DELTA Ministries International (Short-term training and sending Ministry)
Executive Committee for the Standards of Excellence in Short-Term Mission (www.stmstandards.org)

GIVING WISELY?

Jonathan Martin

Last Chapter

Publishing
opening the door to possibilities

GIVING WISELY?
published by Last Chapter Publishing LLC.
© 2008 by Jonathan Martin

International Standard Book Number
0-9816514-0-2

Cover design: Sam Van Diest

For information:
LAST CHAPTER PUBLISHING, LLC
POST OFFICE BOX 1482
SISTERS, OREGON 97759
www.lastchapterpublishing.com

TABLE OF CONTENTS

Dedication

To Laura Jane: my amazing wife and friend of 18 years who gets more beautiful every day that passes. Your love for God and for others continues to challenge and inspire me. Your love for me – well, that just blows my mind. Thanks

Acknowledgements

Thanks Dan and Tambry for letting us follow you through mountains of Rwanda and Burundi and for letting us see the faces of the truly poor and your love for them – and thanks for teaching us how to truly love these brothers and sisters in word and in deed. Shel - for taking us along with you to see the Dorobo Church that you have so helped to stand strong – not on you, but the foundation of Christ. The think tank: Doc Walk, Pat T, Dave D, Dr. Don Smith, Barry A – for helping pound out the RAISE principles. Dr. Val, Dave K, and Ralph and Myrna - for your wisdom and years of experience I could draw from. John Van Diest for your belief and insistence that this message must be in the hands of those who have the resources and want to make a positive and lasting difference in the world. Randy, Marshall, Stu, Bob M, Kathy N - for your time, input, and encouragement. To all the people at Good Shepherd Community Church - when it comes to seeing the need and meeting it – you guys always step up. To all who pray for me and my family. Thanks Darragh, Dannah, and Daylon - for the willing sacrifice of sending me to work with those who are really hurting.

All thanks are to Him who gave everything that we might be transformed and empowered to live and give as we ought.

All proceeds from this book will go to Good Shepherd Community Church's Relief Fund which is dedicated to transforming the lives of the most vulnerable around the world.

If you have questions or comments about giving wisely - please join the discussion on *www.givingwisely.blogspot.com*

Prologue

Oh, the Damage Good Intentions Can Do

Nothing is worse than active ignorance
Johann Wolfgang von Goethe

There is a path which seems right to a man,
But its end is the way of death.
King Solomon

Mexico, 2007: A Mexican orphanage near the U.S. border had figured out how to work the system. American Christians are generous—very generous. But when it comes to the ways they give – they can be a bit uninformed. And this orphanage found it easy to keep them this way.

During the Christmas season, truckloads of gifts arrived for the parentless children. Many U.S churches had heard the call of the Scriptures to help the orphans in their distress, and they responded in the way they'd been trained to respond: Give money; send gifts. Church after church sent truckload after truckload of nice stuff.

As one truck was emptied, the goods were quickly hidden so the next church with their truckload of stuff wouldn't see the vast amount of gifts already received from other generous churches. All the churches were easily kept under the delusion that they were giving the only gifts these poor children would receive. And the orphan children were known by the locals to be the wealthy kids in their neighborhood.

My friend, Walter, who was working for the spiritual well-being of these kids, was amazed at the high quality and vast quantity of gifts being received. He watched as a truckload of very nice football jerseys was unloaded. They all matched with a different number on each jersey. The young men were delighted. The photos taken for the church folk who gave back in the U.S showed joyous beaming smiles. But this delight on their faces was not for the reasons we might simply choose to believe. These young recipients of the gifts knew these jerseys would receive top price in the markets. They already had way too many clothes. Americans love to give clothing.

Hours later, Walter saw these same jerseys in the markets for sale. Cash now in hand, the boys came back to the orphanage. That night Walter noticed these same young men leaving the orphan complex. Curious, he followed and watched as they walked out to meet a truck arriving from the city—arriving with a different kind of Christmas gift. The truck carried several young women. The boys were able to purchase these prostitutes thanks to the generosity of the American churches.

Walter's heart was broken. These were boys he loved. They were being empowered for evil by the very good intentioned, but ignorant, generosity of the church.

* * *

Ouch.

How about a more subtle story:

A group of men from our church heard about a work of God among the extremely poor in a shanty town on the outskirts of Mexico City. In the midst of the plastic roofs and tin walls, many had come to faith, and a church of hundreds had sprung up in a very short time. The church met outside, and the pastor lived in a plastic tent, like the rest in his congregation.

A church should not have to meet this way. A pastor—a man of God—should not have to live this way...

We Americans can fix this problem. A work team...yes, a construction team—let's build them a church building and a small place for the pastor and his family to live. This would be good.

And so it was built, and finished.

And the church was finished. Ruined. Our well-intentioned generous labor of love undermined everything that had been happening there. A year later there was only a handful in this church that had been so alive before the good-intentioned act of generosity.

But how can this be? This makes no sense. The wonderful men on this team came to me trying to make sense of what had happened. So, how did it happen? (Read the rest of the story in chapter 10.)

At first this made no sense to me because I was ignorant about the power of wealth. The power of money to destroy is real. Such good generous men. Such serving hearts. Such hard work. Such carnage. James puts it well, "My brothers, it ought not be this way."

Oh, the horror stories. I have helped write some of them myself. I hear them told time and again. Same song, next verse. So many tragic tales cross my desk. I cry. And I ask myself will these stories ever stop? Most importantly, I ask myself how I can change?

So my quest for a new generosity began. And it continues. It has taken me years to grasp and evaluate this "harmful generosity".

As a result, I have been compelled to not only change myself, but to help others do the same.

And so this book has been written.

But this book isn't just about stopping the physical and spiritual carnage left in the wake of our misguided giving. It's about making our money work to achieve lasting good for the glory and praise of our God.

We're all called to be generous, but we're also all called to be *wise* in our giving—not ignorant or misguided. When it comes to understanding the impact of our generosity upon others, choosing to remain ignorant isn't just slothful and hurtful; it is simply wrong.

The way our money and generosity affects individual lives and whole cultures is indeed a matter of great significance. To continue living in this present state of active ignorance is unacceptable.

Why were we called to be generous in the first place?

We all know the blessings we receive when we give. But I have to seriously ask myself this question: Isn't my generosity really meant to truly bless more than me? Isn't it meant to also bless the one who receives? Great books have been written about why we must be generous for our own sake, but how is it "true generosity" if our gift actually does harm to the one receiving it?

I've spoken to many generous givers who have become disillusioned, and some even cynical, when they see the lack of fruit produced from their generous gift. I've spoken to others who have been destroyed by the very gift they received.

Our giving has got to count. And it must count for good and for eternity. We must not settle merely for the rich blessings we receive. We must truly and eternally bless others with our generosity. To do this, we've got to understand the true value of money and how it can either help or hurt those we give to.

It's *how* we give that makes this difference.

It is my hope that churches, foundations, and generous givers in the west and around the world will start to deeply address these issues. There have been many voices before me saying many of these things. But we need more open dialogue addressing these problems and their solutions. The donors have got to go deep. We have got to give smart.

There are profound principles flowing from the pages of Scripture that we can learn to apply. In a culture that has been given so much, it's time we learn not merely to give—but to give wisely. We must learn to be truly generous.

Part I:
Generosity's True Nature

—

Where Wisdom and Compassion Meet

Chapter One

The Perfect Harvest

A Parable of Thanksgiving

Find out how much God has given you and from it take what you need; the remainder is needed by others.
SAINT AUGUSTINE

A generous man will prosper; he who waters others will himself be watered.
HEBREW PROVERB

This story came to me as I reflected during my first trip to Rwanda. It had not rained for weeks. The crops the people needed for life were wilting in the tropical sun. I thought of the supermarket back home. I could hardly stand it. Why would God allow such inequities?

Maybe this would be the year. Probably not. But maybe. If the weather would just cooperate in a big way. Maybe.

As a nine-year-old I had a dream to go to Disneyland. But the problem was big: Disneyland was out in California, and I lived on a farm in Nebraska. It was a long ways off, and getting there cost more than we could afford.

Disneyland had its grand opening in 1956 when I was four years old, and for my ninth birthday, I asked Dad—like I had on earlier birthdays—"Can we go this year?" He always said, "If the rain comes down just right, and if we get a crop that's just right." So I prayed that this year—1961—those "just right" rains would fall. "God, give us a harvest like never before. Make it perfect."

We owned a couple thousand acres just to the west of Meridian Creek. Across the creek, our friends and neighbors, the Eastmans, owned an almost identical farm. We grew the same crops and raised the same animals. They had four kids, the same ages as those in our family. (One problem: The one my age was a *girl*, Jennifer; all my other siblings had someone their own age and "kind" to play with. Oh well.) The Eastmans also held out the hope for that perfect harvest, so both families together might head out to California and the Big D, as we called it.

> *Right when I finished my prayer, I heard thunder.*

I prayed the weather would be perfect, and at first, it was. My dad called it a perfect winter and spring, leaving the soil just right for planting. The seeds went into the ground, and in no time they were growing. Dad was encouraged. Never had the crops come up so plentiful. I could look down and across Meridian Creek and see the sprouts as beautiful and as plentiful as they'd ever been, both on our land and on the Eastmans' land.

Then, as the days grew hot, a week and a half went by with no rain. We had no irrigation at that time, and one evening Dad said we needed rain now if we were going to have that perfect harvest I'd been praying for. I got nervous. *I'm in danger of losing Disneyland.* I prayed like mad. And right when I finished my prayer, I heard thunder. It was so great.

It poured for about fifteen minutes, soaking everything. Or so I thought. I woke up the next morning and ran out to see our crops. It was beautiful. My dad stood there with me and spoke the words

I wanted to hear: "A perfect rain."

Then we glanced down the hill toward Meridian Creek and the property line we shared with the Eastmans. Dad got a strange look on his face, and started down the hill. I followed out of curiosity. As we got closer to the creek, I could see why he was so puzzled. The soil on the east side of the creek was dry. The storm had poured on our side, but had left our neighbor's farm conspicuously dry. "For some reason," Dad said, "that thunderstorm decided to rain on us, but not the Eastmans. Strange. Boy, they sure need the rain."

Just from that rain alone, our crops jumped way ahead of the Eastmans'. I was happy, because it meant Disneyland for me, but my hopes for the Eastmans coming with us seemed crushed.

Five days later, it rained again. Brilliant lightning. Unbelievable thunder. I loved the sound of the huge raindrops on our roof. They meant life—not only for our crops, but for us as well. It was a soaker. "Perfect," Dad said again. I rejoiced, knowing the Eastmans got the rain they needed to at least keep their crops from dying. I stepped out into the cool air left in the wake of the thunderstorm, and ran down to the creek. To my horror, it had happened again. Their soil was barely damp. The moisture wouldn't even reach the roots of the shallowest of plants. But the rain on our side had never been more "perfect."

I saw Mr. Eastman in his fields checking the soil. Disappointment was all over his face. When his eyes caught mine he walked over and said hi, then invited me along with my whole family over for dinner the next day after church. What a sweet man. They were hurting, but still they gave.

We knew if they didn't get rain in the next few days, their crops were done.

Three days later, we had a perfect rain once again. But not really perfect. I cannot explain how or why, but the Eastmans were again left dry. The whole family was taking buckets from Meridian Creek to water their own personal garden that they'd decided to keep alive right by the creek. It would be enough for their own food, but not enough for their animals or to grow the crops that would pay the bills.

While our crops were the best they'd ever been, I had to watch theirs wither and die on the other side of the creek.

Why were we so blessed while they seemed to be cursed?

Why? Why such strange weather? Why were we so blessed while they seemed to be cursed?

Had they sinned in some way? That question came to my mind. If they had, this would make sense. But the Eastmans were good people. They were leaders in our church. They were all kind. Even Jennifer was kind—sort of—even when I was mean to her. Sin was not the answer.

Were they lazy? If they had been, they would be getting what they deserved. But they were working five times as hard as us to get only one-tenth the amount of crops. They were not lazy.

No matter how I asked the question, I could come up with no good answer.

Harvest time came. "Perfect." That's what Dad said. It was the dream harvest we'd always longed for. It would be double our usual. Our profits would be so great that Dad could get the new tractor he'd wanted, and our trip to Disneyland could become a reality. It was everything I'd dreamed and prayed for.

Except for one very obvious thing.

When I looked down across Meridian Creek, I saw not a dream come true, but a nightmare. A family just like ours, but their livelihood decimated. I sat on the hill overlooking their misfortune. I wanted to be happy about our own success and congratulate our family, but I realized we ultimately had nothing to do with it. It had been the rains. As I looked over the Eastmans' desert-like landscape, I wept.

Dad called a family conference. "Kids, we have the harvest of a lifetime. We need to decide what to do with it. I've promised you all that we'll go to Disneyland. So come winter break, we're off to California!"

The words I'd been living to one day hear. Words which should have been met by the screams of kids so excited they couldn't contain themselves. Words that were instead met with dead silence.

"I thought you kids would be happy. It's our dream come true. What's wrong?"

"They have nothing. Why would God do this? Why give us twice what we need, and give them barely anything at all?"

Of course, Dad knew exactly why we were silent, but he didn't let on.

"Dad," I said. "The Eastmans."

"What about them?"

"Dad, they have nothing. Why would God do this? Why give us twice what we need, and give them barely anything at all?"

"I don't know, honey. Why?"

My question had answered itself. *Twice* what we need; twice what *we* need...

Then it just spilled out of my mouth. "He gave us twice so we could give them half."

I couldn't believe I'd said it. But more than that I couldn't believe the reaction of my brothers. "Yeah. Yeah!" Excitement filled the air. The thought of giving to our neighbors excited us as much as the thought of Disneyland used to.

A few days before Thanksgiving, all of us kids climbed on top of a huge truckload of grain. The first of several we took that day down across Meridian Creek and up to the silos that stood empty next to the Eastmans' house...

I'll never celebrate a Thanksgiving, or hear the word Disneyland, without remembering and seeing Mr. Eastman silently standing there on the bottom step of his porch—that single tear as it fell, clearing a path through the dust on his cheek. And Jennifer's smile as she stood there holding his hand.

It was the perfect harvest.

So why the strange weather patterns? Why such inequities?

I finally understood. If it had rained on both sides of the creek, we would never have known the great joy of giving to those who truly need. And they would have never known the joy of seeing God meet their needs through their neighbors on the other side of the creek. Truly such inequities bring out the most beautiful and valuable thing this life has to offer—and it's not Disneyland—it's a simple thing called love.

Chapter Two

Giving: Where Do We Start?

We make a living by what we get, but we
make a life by what we give.
WINSTON CHURCHILL

So he called ten of his servants and gave
them ten minas. 'Put this money to work,' he
said, 'until I come back.'
JESUS

That story in chapter one may be fiction, but in real sense it is all too true. It's about all of us who have been raised with God's material and spiritual blessings, and about others who are sitting in areas of physical and spiritual famine. It's about those who happened to have been born on a land where there's plenty—where each of labor's seeds returns a hundred-fold—and it's about others who plant twice the seeds, yet receive only one-tenth the harvest. It's about those of us who are granted to sit on the "western" side of the creek, looking across to those who were granted to be born on the other side. It's about a choice whether to chase our economic dreams and "Disneylands," or to step out in faith across the dividing line to help our neighbors.

Why am I in that place on earth where the rains of blessing are abundant?

Why such inequities? We live on a sin-stained planet. Man has made a mess of things. But we must ask ourselves: Why am I in that place on earth where the rains of blessing are abundant?

The answer is before us. The Scriptures shout to us: "To them that are given much, much is required."

Economic inequities are only part of the imbalance. We here in the West have access to biblical training unlike any place in history. We have spiritual resources sitting in bookstores and pouring into our cars and homes over the airwaves. We're a huge storehouse of spiritual and physical food given to us by God for the very purpose of feeding the nations. To hoard these goods is sin. If we don't give generously, something is wrong.

There have been many books written about the biblical case for giving. (Read *The Treasure Principle* by Randy Alcorn. It will become a classic.) The case for giving has been made, and the verdict is in. *Give. Don't wait. Start now.*

The first principle is clear: *GIVE. And give generously.*

But *how* should we give? Are there Biblical principles to apply to our giving?

Jesus told the rich young ruler to sell all his stuff and to give it to the poor. But he didn't tell this guy which of the poor were most deserving. And he didn't say if he should give it as cash or as food or as furniture. He didn't say which organization to give it through. The principle Jesus gave us was clear and remains clear: *Give.*

Jesus takes another step in this direction when he says, "Give to whomever asks of you." Something inside us can be bothered by such an unclear statement. What's this all about? What does he mean? Should we give money to the drunk who asked just so he can go buy more alcohol? Can Jesus really mean that?

I believe Jesus simply means this: Knowing our hearts, and how many of us are prone to find every excuse under the sun for *not* giving to a person or church or organization, he simply says, "Give." *It's better to give to a poorly run organization, or to a drunken bum who in turn goes and buys more booze, than to be selfish and not give at all.*

I had a friend once who had real reservations about giving to his home church because he didn't agree with the way the money was being spent. He was a successful businessman and made good money; and though I never checked his giving record, I really wonder if he was giving to the church at all. I also heard him give many reasons for not giving to this missionary or that missionary because he felt the amount of money they were asked to raise was too much. Besides, the ten percent overhead the organization scraped off the top was ridiculous. Needless to say, when my wife and I left for the mission field with our kids, this close businessman friend was not one of our supporters.

The last time we got together, he made this statement, "You know, I feel like I'll never be really financially free until I have more than a million dollars in the bank."

Now I cannot be sure – just a hunch of mine, but I suspect that the problems he found at the church and with organizations were used as justification not to give. Jesus gives us an answer to those of us who are quick to find fault and slow to give. His answer: "Give!"

If you're waiting for perfection before you give —you'll never give.

Does that mean we should give foolishly and not be good stewards? No, not at all. But it does mean there's no perfect way to give your money. Some churches are more responsible than others, but none is perfect. No missionary organization is perfect either. No missionary you might support is perfect. If you're waiting for perfection before you give—you'll never give, you'll never be generous, and you'll always live in your selfishness and greed.

So—*give generously.*

But there's a second biblical principle that's just as important. When we give generously, we're responsible to invest *wisely.*

So where do we start investing? Here at home or where the need is greatest? Should I tithe locally to my church when we have so much excess here in this country and in other countries people are dying?

Hey, I'm a missionary. I have the heart of a missionary and the independent spirit that goes along with one, too. I've studied and watched how we Christians spend money. I cringe at times when I hear the cost of things my own church purchases. In my mind, I take the $40,000 spent on a piece of sound equipment, and I calculate how many lives could have been saved with that money. Quite a few. You might be like me.

So what's the answer? Do I send my tithe overseas? Do I just withhold half of that ten percent from my local church, and give directly to missions and the poor?

> *Yes, I use to believe that I was the enlightened one, and the elders and leaders in my church were not.*

Many people I know do exactly that. I used to be one of them. Yes, I once believed that I was the enlightened one, and the elders and leaders in my church were not. I believed in the principle of the tithe, so I gave, but it was up to me to decide where it went. After all—I was "enlightened."

Actually, *proud* is what I was. And I had a problem with authority. Another principle in the Scriptures is "submit to those in authority." I realized in my heart that if I was committed to attend a church and to minister there, but held back from giving to that local body, then I was being a proud, "enlightened" rebel; and I wasn't submitting to a God-given authority in my life.

Just as in the book of Acts, the people brought their money to the apostles and trusted them to distribute the money to those in need—so I needed to learn to trust those in authority. If we can not trust the local church here where we can see it and be involved in it, then what right do we have to invest and trust the local church to do good on the other side of the planet? The local church – it is God's chosen agent of change. We have got to get behind it here – and there.

I believe God wanted to teach me how to lead by following those in charge, even though I couldn't agree with all their financial decisions. God has blessed that decision to give my first ten percent locally, and has enabled us to give beyond that to the desperate needs around the world. I also thank God my church is giving away a huge chunk of what I give. In fact, some sixteen years after making that decision to give that ten percent to our church, I see how God has used our church to support my own family—roughly 40 percent of our needs while we were in East Asia.

Now I'm home serving at that very church, overseeing their global outreach—and I find myself involved in deciding where to give close to a million dollars a year that the church has channeled toward missions and the poor. Ironically, I now find myself wanting to get people to tithe locally so we can give more away to folks who really need it overseas.

That being said, there's a real problem with a church that doesn't give to reach the world and the desperate needs that exist out there. If I belonged to such a church, I would have to be an activist working to warm and soften this cold, calloused heart— for "whoever has the world's goods, and sees his brother in need and closes his heart against him, how does the love of God abide in him?" Such an unchristian policy must be changed.

If that church refused to change, there would be a dilemma; but I wouldn't stop tithing. Instead, I would stop going to that church. I would find a church that had the "love of Christ abiding in it" and that was taking steps in the right direction—which means generously giving to those around the world who have yet to hear the gospel, and to those places where our brothers and sisters are starving, dying, and struggling to stay alive in war-torn areas. I would throw in my first fruits with this church and try to influence and shape them even more in that direction.

We've been given so much, and to keep it all to feed our own "fat" selves—well, there's no excuse for that. I cannot help but think God himself gets angry when some new church says they need all the funds for themselves until they get to be such and such a size. There's a principle at work here: If you start your church with a selfish heart, you can only guess where that will take you.

If you start your church with a selfish heart, you can only guess where that will take you.

A good friend of mine planted a church just two years ago. The first two weeks of services, the offerings were completely given away to the needy. More than $16,000. The church has been going for just two years, and in its second year it gave away $295,492— nearly 45 percent of its total budget.

Here's a quotation from that pastor who helped to start this church:

> Christ laid out his priorities in Luke 4:18-19. He said his first "target audience" for the good news would be the poor, the imprisoned, the blind, and the downtrodden. The way the church uses money should reflect Christ's priorities.
>
> Most of the people who attend our local church are not imprisoned, poor, blind, and downtrodden. That means we have to look outside the church to other ministries and organizations we can give money to — and we do this before we spend money on ourselves.
> Pastors love to quote Malachi 3:10 — "Bring the whole tithe into the storehouse" — but then they quickly abandon the analogy. A storehouse is a temporary stopover for a commodity (in this case money). Imagine if a Home Depot manager decided that instead of pushing sales out the front door, he would use ninety percent of the products coming in the back doors to enlarge and beautify his store, and he did this for years and years. What a fantastic "Home Depot Campus" he would create! The idea, of course, is ludicrous. Yet, it's exactly what many American churches are doing.

If any group had that right to keep some money until they had enough to give away, it's a new church plant—right? No, Jesus praised the widow who, in her poverty did not keep her last few cents, but gave it away (Mark 12:41-44).

Jesus is very clear: We're to take the message of the gospel in word and in deed to all nations. Our money needs to fund this. Jesus also says to take care of the poor—the least of these. Our money needs to fund these non-negotiable parts of the gospel as well.

In a nation where we have so much, there's a lot of confusion about what this means to fund the gospel, and to help the poor.

Giving Generously, Investing Wisely—It's Got to Be Both

> There are a thousand hacking at the branches of evil to one who is striking at the root. (Thoreau)

> Do not be deceived: God cannot be mocked. Whatever a man sow that will he reap. (Paul the apostle)

Imagine that your boss gives you $1,000 in crisp twenty-dollar bills to invest for him. Which of the following outcomes would bring your boss the most pleasure? And which would bring him the most anger?

1. You think, research, plan, invest, and one year later you've doubled your investment. *You hand your boss $2,000.*

2. You stick the money under your mattress, and a year later you hand him back the same crisp bills he gave you. *You hand your boss $1,000.*

3. You put the money in the bank and gain interest. At today's present interest rates, you don't make much. *You hand your boss $1,001.*

4. You make various investments based on emotional appeals, and a sense of duty and/or guilt. These investments (though you're not aware of this) dehumanize people, cause disunity, feed corruption, and create dependency. Plus, you end up in the red. *You ask your boss to pay off a debt of $500.*

Naturally, a human boss would be most satisfied with outcome #1, the greatest return on his dollars.

And he would probably be most angry at outcome #4, because you put him in debt. But then, God is different from earthly bosses (thank goodness). So *is it wrong to be appealed to emotionally?* After all, we're emotional beings. *Is it wrong to give because of guilt?* Certainly there are better reasons to give, but there are a few times in my own life that, quite frankly, it did me some good to feel guilty enough to give, and I should have felt guilty if I hadn't given. *Is it wrong to have a sense of duty toward God?* Of course not.

Besides, all those poor investments could have just been a case of beginner's bad luck. At least in #4, you tried to do what the boss told you.

> All of us should aspire to be the one who gives back $2,000 to the boss.

I believe God gets most angry with us in outcome #2—when we only bury what he has given us to invest. That's exactly what makes "the master" angry in the parable Jesus told in Matthew 25.

But here's the point: All of us should aspire to be the one who gives the boss back $2,000. We should want to invest wisely.

But there's much more to wise investment than good intentions and generous hearts.

It's all about investing *wisely*—not just giving away a bunch of money.

So, number one: *Give and give generously.* This is a non-negotiable part of being a believer in Jesus.

And number two: *Give wisely.* We're to make our investment count.

Wise and Foolish Generosity—A Parable

How quickly nature falls into revolt when gold becomes her object! (William Shakespeare)

Of what value is money when in the hand of a fool, since he has no heart to attain wisdom? (Ancient Hebrew Proverb)

Day One

Two very generous men approached the old bridge that crossed the river. The generous man on the left looked down to his left and saw a thin man in tattered clothing frantically grabbing at the river with his bare hands. The generous man on the right looked down the right side of the bridge and saw an almost identical scene of a poorly clothed, extremely scrawny man spastically grabbing and slapping at the water and even occasionally going clear under for several seconds at a time.

The generous man on the left climbed down to the poor guy and inquired, "What exactly are you doing?"

"I am a poor man with a wife and many children to feed. I am trying to catch some fish to feed them."

"Well, you're never going to catch any with your bare hands! Here's twenty dollars. Go buy your family some food."

The poor man had never seen so much money in his life. "Thank you. You're the kindest man I've ever met," he said, as he hugged the generous man. He then ran to the market and bought for his family something they'd never had before. A feast. They were royalty for an evening, all because of the generosity of a man.

The generous man on the right climbed down the bank to the

poor man on his side. Upon inquiring, he found out the exact same thing: "I'm a poor man with a wife and children to feed," etc.

When the words of this sad story fell upon the ears of this generous man, he told the poor man to wait there. He climbed back up the bank, and headed into town. He soon returned with a fishing pole. He sat down next to the man, and for the next several hours helped him perfect his fishing. Soon the poor man had pulled in several large trout.

After receiving a simple but very pleasant, "Thank you," this generous man departed for his home.

Day Two

The next day at the same time the same two generous men came to the same bridge where they were the day before.

The man on the left looked down and saw the same man trying to catch fish with the same bare hands. The same thing happened as the day before: He gave the man twenty dollars.

The man on the right also looked down and saw the same man —yet he wasn't the same, for there he sat with his fishing pole and a small pile of fish by his side. This generous man chatted with his new friend, gave him more fishing pointers, then headed up the river to see who else he could help.

Day Three

It was almost the same scenario for the generous man on the left. But instead of there being one man trying to catch fish with his hands, there were two—and they were just sitting, not trying to catch fish, looking over their shoulders as though they expected someone to come to help. The generous man gave each man twenty dollars. The men thanked him, and left.

The generous man on the right again went up stream, gave another fishing pole away, and taught another man how to fish.

Day Four

The generous man on the left didn't even have to look down the bank. There were four poor men standing there on the road with wet hands. They told him they'd been trying to catch fish with no luck. Once again the generous man gave each a generous gift, and they were off.

The generous man on the right went upstream this day to teach yet another to fish, but this time he took the man he'd met on the first day, and had him do the teaching.

Day Five

The generous man on the left couldn't even step out of his home, for there was a sizable crowd of people at his door, telling him how they could catch no fish that day. Suddenly, this very generous man, for the first time in his life, did not feel very generous at all.

The generous man on the right stayed in town this day teaching several poor people to tie flies and how to make fly-fishing poles. There they sat with eager faces, learning a trade that would empower them to provide for their families. As this generous man looked at the satisfaction on their faces, he felt very generous indeed.

Both men will be rewarded for their giving and generous intentions, but only the one will be rewarded for his wisdom and good works.

Chapter Three

Does Money Make the Gospel Go 'Round?

We ought to change the legend on our money
from "In God We Trust" to "In Money We
Trust." Because, as a nation, we've got far
more faith in money these days than we do in
God.

ARTHUR HOPPE

Some men worship rank, some worship
heroes, some worship power, some worship
God, and over these ideals they dispute; but
they all worship money.

MARK TWAIN

You were sold for nothing, and without money
you will be redeemed.

ISAIAH

The apostle Paul, along with a few others, took the gospel throughout the Roman Empire. From city to city he took the good news, and the few he led to Christ would lead many others to faith. The gospel spread like wildfire. This area of the world was the cradle of Christianity.

I often wonder what we, as modernized Americans, would think if we could step into this world of the first century.

Our first impression would likely be nausea from the stench. Though the city of Rome had one of the most advanced sewage systems of the time, it was a far cry from what we have today, and even the best Roman city would reek with a smell we identify today with the third world.

Most people in the Roman Empire lived in small villages in small houses with families packed together in close quarters. Their outhouse (if you could call it that) was out back and ripe. In the cities, there were animals pulling carts and leaving their stuff in the streets. Indeed, most cities were extremely unsanitary, backward and poor by our standards.

Transportation was slow, primitive, and extremely dangerous. Even the wealthy lived in homes where they were cold in the winter with poor heating at best, and they had to spend their evenings without electricity and in darkness barely lit with small oil lamps. Imagine a three-watt bulb.

Most homes in the empire were simple and made of stones and mud. Floors were commonly dirt, or if they were wealthy—stone. There was no refrigeration; once prepared, food had to be eaten on the spot.

Roads, even in the cleanest cities, were dusty and dirty by our modern western standards. The famous Roman baths, as nice as they're made to look in the movies, would have disgusted any westerner and would be seen as primitive by our modern standards. Imagine, hundreds bathing all in the same untreated water all day long—and the water sometimes not changed for days. Yuck. Health departments today would have closed them in an instant.

Many of those who were very well-to-do in that ancient

society we would classify as very poor today. I, for one, would feel great sympathy for those having to live that way. Imagine no air conditioning or even an electric fan on a brutally hot and humid summer day.

Actually, most everything in that culture, with the exception of the great architectural structures of Greece and Rome, would seem to us to be extremely third world, and we modern Americans would classify nearly all people of that time as poor.

> It was here, in this poverty, that Christianity was born and grew. Nothing could stop it.

Yet it was here, in this poverty, that Christianity was born and grew. Nothing could stop it.

So here's the question: *Were our American dollars needed to spread the gospel?*

And yet another question: *Does someone who lives without electricity, refrigeration, pizza, television, and plumbing need our money so they can modernize and be happy?*

Our church culture of the West resoundingly answers "yes" to both questions. We often unknowingly have a condescending attitude towards those in the third world. And that attitude is reflected in this thought: "*These people cannot spread the gospel without my money.*" But the fact is, Christians did it in the first century, and they can do it now.

> No one is poor just because he lives simply.

They're very capable, intelligent, hardworking, gifted people, and their desire to please God is often greater than ours.

"Yes," we say, "but these people are so poor. They need my help." The fact is, they often are eating decent diets, have enough clothes, and have a roof over their heads. And they actually have time for important things like relationships with family and friends, plus time to share the message of the gospel with others. Their resulting psychological well-being is often far superior to that of our own people in this culture. No one is poor just because he lives simply.

Just a few nights ago, I sat in a crowded living room filled with college-age kids and young couples. They'd asked me to come over and talk on the topic of this book. As I sat there, I asked them, "Is this weekly meeting a meaningful time of ministry for you all?" I already knew what they would answer. This group was tight. They'd been through a lot with each other. They loved each other deeply, and they loved Jesus and studying his word.

"It's the greatest!" came their reply.

My next question was this: "How much money did it take to make this evening happen?"

"Bree and her parents made dinner for us, and that cost," they replied.

"And next week, another one of you will do dinner—right?" I asked.

They agreed.

"So if you keep taking turns you don't spend any more money than you would if you each fed yourself—right? But it's more convenient to have one make for all."

"Yeah," came their reply.

"So it really didn't take any extra money to make very meaningful ministry take place. Is that right?

They all agreed.

This point cannot be overemphasized. The most meaningful kinds of ministry can be done without extra money. The kind of ministry that changed the Roman Empire in the first century was done just like this. And today, arguably the greatest awakening in the history of this planet is the explosion of China's house ministry —where ministry is done just like this. The leaders of most of these churches work an eight-to-five job, the people come together in homes, and the burden of the food cost is shared. With the exception of buying Bibles, there's virtually no overhead. Much of the church's giving goes not toward the paying of professionals, but toward sending some of their own out to the next town to reach others.

As I was sharing with this group of young Christians, one of them asked. "So why is ministry in America so different and so dependent on money?"

Without really even thinking I replied. "What's our number one natural resource as Americans?"

"Money," they replied

"So it makes sense," I explained, "that in a culture where we're so used to spending exorbitant amounts of money on everything, this habit would carry over into our churches. It's part of our culture. It's no big deal to throw down two hundred dollars for our high school weekend retreat going on this weekend, is it? And this retreat is a good thing. But we soon come to believe that this is the way people are reached with the gospel—because that's how we've always seen it done, and it has worked. So we export this kind of ministry technique to cultures that don't throw money at everything. And what do you think happens?"

They knew. "We mess up their culture and the culture of their church."

What could have and perhaps would have spread just fine *without* the use of dollars, we westerners show others how to do only *with* dollars.

What would have spread just fine without the use of dollars, we westerners show others how to do only with dollars.

But it takes *American* dollars, because they don't have this kind of money or this kind of culture.

We have, as well-intentioned generous Americans, sewn the first seeds of dependency, and thus have almost guaranteed that their church can grow only as big as our western bucks can take it.

My brethren, it ought not be this way.

Am I saying there's no need then to give? As Paul would put it, "May it never be!" Jesus said we must give. There are those in desperate need who go without the basic needs of life. And it's true, there are those who can and will be reached with the gospel through our wise investments, and who otherwise wouldn't have a chance to hear and believe. But the attitude that we're in some way superior because of our "advanced" culture and "superior" ways is the wrong place to start. These "poor" people have just as much to offer us—maybe even more—than we have for them. The idea that it's money (especially the American dollar) that makes the gospel go 'round is ludicrous and destructive.

So please listen well: The good news is spread by *people in relationships.* And *it's the power of the Holy Spirit that brings it home.* It has always been this way, and it will remain this way until Jesus comes back.

Money has as great a potential to destroy as it does to save; and our attitude and the resulting way in which we give has also the power to build or tear down.

Money is a lot like fire. When controlled and used wisely, its potential for good is enormous. But when it burns outside certain parameters, its power to destroy is unmatched. We Christians in the West turn money loose on those we're supposed to help outside the boundaries that are meant for it —and it burns them badly, often more than it helps. We must know the boundaries. We must keep the fire in its place.

> *Money is a lot like fire. When controlled and used wisely, its potential for good is enormous. But when it burns out of certain set parameters, its power to destroy is unmatched.*

Did the early church of the first century need someone from a "rich country" to start writing checks so they could spread the gospel? Did the early church need someone to come in and build them a nice church building so they could disciple others?

The answer of course is no. So before we run in and do that very thing, we need to stop and ask, "Is this the best way to spend our time and money? Does this use of our money best foster the relationships that spread the good news of Christ?" Maybe building a church building is the best use of our money. But then again, there may be something far superior. The point is: *We must not just assume our western ways are the best!*

Did the pastors of the early churches need cars to go from town to town to spread the gospel? The answer of course is no. They got around the same way the other locals did. Imagine that—the gospel can be spread on foot! That's hard for us westerners to imagine, seeing as how some of us drive a hundred yards down the street to the store to get a gallon of milk. So we western churches are buying cars all the time for our third world brothers and pastors, elevating them to the level of the "extremely rich" in their culture—all for the cause of spreading the gospel, which could have been done in that culture much better on foot. There's a verse somewhere about that. Oh yes: "How lovely are the feet of him who brings good news." Imagine that—*lovely feet*. A lovely car; now, I understand that one. Again, it's this cultural misunderstanding of ours: *"We* need cars, so they must too."

Did the pastors of churches in the Roman Empire need support from America to make ends meet? No. Do we need to dump an extra $300 a month on a rural third world pastor? Perhaps if our motivation is to appease the guilt we feel for living in a home six times the size of his humble place. But by such "generous" giving, we elevate this pastor high above the rest of his congregation—ruining his rapport with his people, and almost *guaranteeing they'll never tithe again.* And, hey—a one- or two-room house is not a bad thing! It offers great protection from the rain and cold, and people have loved living in them for thousands of years. Maybe, instead of appeasing our guilt by giving generously but in such a harmful way for the gospel, we should ask ourselves if we really need those ten rooms for our family of four. In our culture that would take some real thought.

So, What Is Poverty?

We have to realize that poverty doesn't mean the absence of big houses and fancy cars. The simple lifestyle—free from cars, TVs, gadgets, and processed foods—does not mean the poor life.

The Bible never says anything about getting bigger houses and more things for people who are already provided for, but who happen to be living simply. It does however talk about caring for

44

the widow, the orphan, and the refugee, and fighting for the rights of the oppressed—all of whom have an inadequate way of meeting their genuine needs. We need to be concerned about those who cannot take care of themselves— the hungry, the thirsty, the sick, the dying, those who are alone.

Our giving can help advance the good news of the kingdom, but it doesn't do so just because it's money, or just because we're generous with it.

And the whole message of the Bible is that people have need of a Savior. We must be concerned about those who are spiritually destitute as well—those who are alone in the prison of self, and all those who have never heard the message of Jesus.

Our giving can make a difference. It can help advance the good news of the kingdom, but it doesn't do so *just* because it's money, or *just* because we're generous with it.

Spiritual and physical poverty is never done away with by the simple writing of a check. It must be done through a relationship filled with love, patience, wisdom, and understanding—with the goal of change lasting not merely for a day, a year, or even a lifetime, but for all of eternity. And we ourselves must be directly involved in these kinds of relationships.

Money should never be thought of as a substitute for our own engagement in the relationships that change lives.

Money should never be thought of as a substitute for our own engagement in the relationships that change lives. And if our money isn't flowing through channels that foster these relationships of love, patience, wisdom, and understanding with that eternal goal in mind, we might as well just fly over poor countries where many have yet to hear the gospel and airdrop all our cash.

GIVING WISELY?

Chapter Four

Ending Poverty

It's easy to make a buck. It's a lot tougher to
make a difference.
TOM BROKAW

Rich and poor have this much in common:
The Lord God is the Maker of them all.

KING SOLOMON

Ending poverty. This is a noble goal. Bono sings about it.
Governments talk about it. Churches pray for it.

Indeed it would be nice for poverty to end. The communists
had their unique way to end poverty, and that was simply to make
everyone equally poor—and as long as they didn't know any better,
they might be happy. It could have worked just fine, except for the
fact that they lived in an information age where they could see that
others elsewhere were becoming wealthier.

What does it mean to be poor? When does someone become
rich? In America, folks are officially declared to be poor when they
are living at or below the "poverty line" - most recently defined
as living on $21,200 for a family of four, yet they have their big-
screen TV and are fifty pounds overweight. Is that poor? By whose
standard?

Those considered rich in one culture are considered poor by
another.

In Sudan, the people of the Dinka tribe measure their wealth

6
GIVING WISELY ?

in their number of cattle. There was an extremely rich Dinka who
had several hundred head of cattle,
and because of this wealth, he
held a special place of prominence
and authority in his culture. Also
because of his wealth, this six-foot-
four man -a common height among the Dinka - weighs close to
two hundred pounds, and is called fat by those around him which
is a great compliment in that culture. His home is made of sticks
and mud, and has a grass roof. He is without electricity. His small
two-room house (made of two grass huts adjoined for a total of
900 square feet for his family of six) has within it the only item
we westerners might find familiar – a small iron cooking pot. He
wears what looks like blankets wrapped around his body, which are
woven with the wool from his own sheep. He wears sandals made
from the hide of his own cattle. He feels proud. He's a rich man.
And he knows it.

Those considered rich in one culture are considered poor by another.

Suddenly there's a noise. A rumble. It's a car. It pulls to a stop
in front of his home. Out of the car hops another Sudanese—an old
friend—back from the city in a neighboring country where he has
made his fortune. This man is fat, and like most of us here in the
West, a nice belly is hanging over his belt. He greets his rich friend
—the cattleman.

The rich cattleman looks at this car. He looks at the watch on
this guy's wrist. He notices the rings on the fingers and the necklace
around his friend's neck. He looks at the colorful clothes on his
back and the pants with a fancy and belt and buckle. The shirt is
tucked in showing off that trophy of a belly.

Everything just changed. Suddenly, the cattleman is not rich at all.

He feels ashamed. He's a poor man. And he knows it.

Suppose Bill Gates walked into my home of 2,000 square feet. He'd see a three-year-old computer and a ten-inch television that's fifteen years old. Out in the driveway, he couldn't help noticing that we drive two cars, both with more than 100,000 miles and a few dents. He might indeed feel sorry for me. But the fact that Bill Gates feels sorry for me doesn't make me poor. Actually, it says more about how rich he is. And though I might love to be the object of his compassion, I'm in no way in need. (Well, I could use a Humvee, come to think of it.)

In the same way, I may walk into a house in Northwest China that's home to a family of eight Uighurs (a Muslim nationality) who live in a space of roughly 1,000 square feet. They have no car, but instead commute into town on a donkey cart. I may feel sorry for them, but again, that in no way makes them poor; it simply says something about my materialistic values.

What we've seen is this: I'm poorer than Bill Gates, but I'm not poor; and the Uighur family I'm thinking of is poorer than I am, but that doesn't mean they're poor either. In fact, they're quite well off in their society.

> *My feeling sorry for them in no way makes them poor; it simply says something about my materialistic values.*

So what is *poor*? What is *rich*? Does Einstein's theory of relativity apply here as well? It's critical that before we go around feeling sorry for the poor and giving money to them, we need to decide who it is that's really poor.

Is being poor just a matter of degree—someone has more money and/or possessions than another? The Bible answers with what I believe to be an emphatic no. "With food and clothing I will be content" (1 Timothy 6:8). The Bible's answer is that "enough" means we're being fed and covered or protected from the elements. When food isn't adequate, that's poverty. When we're not clothed, we're poor. When there's no shelter from the cold, the rain, and the sun, where the surroundings are causing disease and death, and where there's no means to care for the sick and dying—this is physical poverty.

> *A recurring theme in the Bible is our obligation to care of those who cannot care for themselves. The widow. The orphan. The alien. The oppressed. The sick.*

A recurring theme in the Bible is our obligation to care of those who cannot care for themselves. The widow. The orphan. The alien. The oppressed. The sick.

The Widow

This woman has lost all means by which to care for herself. She's alone. She bears the weight of both providing for and caring for the children. Because of her circumstances in life, she's usually financially poor, but she's relationally impoverished as well.

There is a spiritual picture here. The marriage relationship is meant to reflect the relationship between Christ and the church; when a woman loses her husband this picture is ripped in two. In our culture, divorce leaves women extremely vulnerable. It's then that the body of Christ must step in and be Christ to that woman. It's not a suggestion; the Bible screams at us. It's something we *must* do.

The Orphan

Like the widow, this child has been deprived of that which is most critical for his well-being. The father and mother being taken away is analogous to God the Father being taken away from his children, the Church. This parent-child relationship is sacred, and when it ceases to be, the church must step in and act. These children must be cared for, or they'll never have a picture of a heavenly Father. The orphan is truly needy.

AIDS is producing more orphans than we can imagine — particularly in Africa. We need to be involved in finding culturally fitting ways to do all we can to make sure these children are cared for. Often our compassion can override our wisdom, but the same principles of RAISE (continue reading to see these principles defined) apply here as well. Any time we can empower locals to take care of locals and make this sustainable, our dollar has been invested for the greatest return.

Never underestimate a people's ability to care for their own — after all, they have the knowledge needed to make it in that culture, and we don't. They *want* to make it — but they often just need help to get off the ground; when they get that help — watch them fly.

I've been amazed at how the local church in Burundi and Rwanda — two of the poorest countries in the world — can be empowered to take care of their own orphans. Our money can be well invested in such projects that create jobs giving income to such children. There are Christian organizations that are working through the local churches to truly empower them to take care of and empower the fatherless.

The Refugee/Alien

While the widow is without her groom, and the orphan without his father and mother, the refugee is without his home.

Again, there's something sacred in the word "home." In the Scriptures, the word *alien* refers to those who came to Israel homeless—often as result of the instability, persecution, war, and famine in their own land. Sometimes these people were just passing through, and sometimes they would come to stay. In both instances the people of Israel were told to take them in. If they were looking for a home, it was the responsibility of the people of Israel to make sure they were given opportunities to work and care for themselves. (The Book of Ruth.)

God's heart breaks for such people. So must ours.

There are perhaps no more forlorn and forsaken people than those who've experienced the ravages of war and must flee the death around them, to become refugees in a country and place not their own. There are many of these who live among us, right here in our own country. God's heart breaks for such people. So must ours. Our people and our dollars need to be at work in these seemingly forsaken places and among these forgotten peoples.

The Oppressed

These are people who have been robbed of justice. Those who are enslaved may be well fed, and may have a roof over their heads, but they're classified by God along with the physically needy. These are the prostitutes held in bondage by their pimps. These are the children forced into labor or sold as sex slaves. These are the believers who've been thrown into prison and who are violently persecuted because of their testimony. Jesus says we're to visit them, which in our country means doing all we can to make sure there's justice on their behalf. There are Christians who have founded organizations committed to fighting these injustices. Our churches need to partner with these groups who are taking our Lord at his word. Our money can be well spent here—on that which is close to the heart of God.

The Truly Poor: The Hungry, Thirsty, and Sick

> We know love by this, that He laid down His life for us; and we ought to lay down our lives for the brethren. But whoever has the world's goods, and sees his brother in need and closes his heart against him, how does the love of God abide in him? Little children, let us not love with word or with tongue, but in deed and truth. (1 John 3:16-18)

If our brothers and sisters are starving and dying from disease, and our overflowing resources can save their lives, yet we turn our eyes and do nothing—well, the apostle John questions our very salvation. "How does the love of God abide in him?" he asks.

The obvious answer to this rhetorical question is, "It does not." It's not an option to turn the other way. We must act.

> For I was hungry, and you gave Me something to eat; I was thirsty, and you gave Me something to drink; I was a stranger, and you invited Me in; naked, and you clothed Me; I was sick, and you visited Me; I was in prison, and you came to Me. (Jesus, in Matthew 25:35-36)

Jesus gave his life for us while we were in such a spiritual state. And if we are of him, we will act. Both Jesus and John make this quite clear.

Churches that don't actively take on these issues - well, Jesus has some strong words for them.

Chapter Five

The High Cost of a Free Lunch

The Theology of Work

There is no use whatever trying to help people
who do not wish to help themselves. You
cannot push anyone up a ladder unless he is
willing to climb it himself.

ANDREW CARNEGIE

For when we were with you,
we gave you this rule: "If a man will not work,
then neither shall he eat."

PAUL THE APOSTLE

Perhaps the most dehumanizing thing you can do to a person is to take away his need to work.

One of the most insidious and destructive things that can happen to a culture is for a government to step in and pay people for being idle. It's a sad thing, but it's human nature to take the low road when it comes to work. Generally, we humans won't learn to work and come to a point of actually enjoying it unless necessity first compels us to work.

> One of the most insidious and destructive things that can happen to a culture is for a government to step in and pay people for being idle.

I remember well spending a couple of days in Montana's glorious

Glacier National Park with my dad and two brothers about a decade ago. We'd been fishing and hiking and enjoying the incredible lodges of the park. The little resort towns of St. Mary's and East Glacier were charming.

We dropped out of the mountains through the pines and aspen in the foothills and drove out to the edge of the Great Plains. We rolled into the small town of Browning. We were planning to eat dinner there, and we were hungry. I expected a cute and cozy town, well fed by eastern tourists flocking to and from the park. What welcomed us were buildings in disrepair, mangy dogs, homes with weeds for lawns, and many houses with boards for windows. We were now on an Indian reservation. There was a Subway sandwich shop on our right. We stopped for dinner.

I was very surprised to find that the Subway restaurant was managed and run by whites. We popped across the street to the local grocery store—again, the majority were whites working in the place. Wasn't this an Indian reservation? What's the deal with the whites running and working the stores? It wasn't till years later that I came to understand the picture more fully.

I spent a chunk of last summer leading a church group of some twenty-five high schoolers to do outreach in this same small town. Astonishingly, the grocery stores, the gas stations, the restaurants are almost all run by non-native Americans. This is true with the casinos and resorts popping up on all of the Native American reservations. Drop in sometime. Notice all the white faces in the positions of employment.

While we were staying on this reservation in Montana, the young people from our church helped a family who owned a small Mexican restaurant. This was one of the few Native American businesses on the entire reservation. We helped the owners, Helen and Jack, paint the entire inside and completely cleaned their restaurant.

I peppered them with a thousand questions about running a business there. I found out that it's relatively easy to get a business going—not a lot of red tape at all. They're not under the watchful eye of the state health bureau, so they're not worried about being shut down by some bureaucracy. It seemed like a friendly place to get a business started. As we worked, we also saw that business was good. People were dropping by all the time to pick up their daily orders of this and that, and others were coming in to sit down to eat. Their clientele was all local. They were running a profitable business.

So easy to start, low bureaucracy, profitable. Sounds great.

So why were we, a church group from Oregon, helping them clean and paint the place? In Helen's words: "Thank you guys so much for helping us paint. We cannot find anyone around here who will do this kind of work." I was a bit shocked. Unemployment on the reservation was right at 70 percent.

"Thank you guys so much for helping us paint this place. We cannot find anyone around here who will do this kind of work." I was a bit shocked. Unemployment on the reservation was right at 70 percent.

I thought we were helping them because they didn't have enough money to pay for help. But they said they had the money to pay someone; there just wasn't any help to be found.

Helen went on, "Yes, we just got back from visiting our daughter and grandkids in California. We had to shut down the restaurant for the two weeks we were gone. We just can't find reliable help that will run the place while we're away. The first year, the guys we hired never showed up for work. The next year they stole from the restaurant while we were gone, so we just decided it was cheaper to close everything when we travel. We lose money, but not as much as if we try to hire someone around here to run it."

"How long have you had the restaurant?" I inquired.

"We've been open for about five years now." Jack replied.

"How many different people have you had working for you?" I asked, thinking that perhaps they hadn't given enough people a chance.

"Oh, probably eighty. But they usually just work until they get one paycheck, and then they don't ever come back. Some just disappear and don't call, and then they show up two weeks later and say they'd just gone down to Billings to visit family."

"What's the longest you've had someone working here?" I asked.

"One girl, she worked for two months. But then she just disappeared." Helen replied.

"Why is it so hard to find good help?"

"Nobody wants to work. The work ethic has been lost around here. They don't know what it means to be responsible. They don't want to work, because they don't have to work."

I asked the pastor of the church in the town what the alcoholism rate is on the reservation. "At least 90 percent of the men are alcoholic. I was too, until Jesus got hold of my life."

My heart was grieved to see the state of affairs among the Native American population. And I realize that I, too, would be just the same if I'd grown up being taken care of by the government. There isn't much incentive to work when you haven't seen it modeled, when idleness is rewarded and when your rent goes up if you go back to work – the more you make, the higher your rent.

It's human nature that we work when we have to. When we have to work in order to eat and put a roof over our heads, then we work—and we often find something very rewarding in the work itself.

> *It's human nature that we work when we have to.*

But the new jobs haven't reduced unemployment for Indians. One analysis found that tribes with established casinos saw their unemployment rate rise four-tenths of a point to 54.4 percent between 1991 and 1997. Jacob Coin, former executive director of the National Indian Gaming Association, said that's because 75 percent of the jobs in tribal casinos are held by non-Indians.

At the Fort Mojave Indian Reservation along the California-Arizona-Nevada border, the unemployment rate climbed from 27.2 percent in 1991 to 74.2 percent in 1997. Tribal administrator Gary Goforth acknowledged that few of the 675 jobs at the tribe's two financially troubled casinos are filled by tribal members. Not everybody wants to be a dealer, or a housekeeper, or even a manager in the restaurant, he said.

We white people have committed a lot of wrongdoing against the Native American peoples. We broke treaties. We stole their once vast territories. And we pushed them onto tattered remnants of land that in no way could support their way of life.

All these were bad enough. But none of these can compare to

what we did next.

Perhaps because of the guilt we felt as a country, we decided to make up for it. As a kind of penance, we decided to pay them to sit there on this land and do nothing. This was, in effect, worse than any of the crimes we'd committed before, for we robbed them of their will to work. By taking away the need to work, we took from them a major component which makes us all human, and which gives man dignity and self respect—a simple thing called *work*.

The Scriptures have some pretty strong words about work:

> He also who is slack in his work is brother to him who destroys. (Proverbs 18:9)

> The desire of the sluggard puts him to death, for his hands refuse to work; (Proverbs 21:25)

> I passed by the field of the sluggard and by the vineyard of the man lacking sense, and behold, it was completely overgrown with thistles; its surface was covered with nettles, and its stone wall was broken down. (Proverbs 24:30-31)

> For you yourselves know how you ought to follow our example, because we did not act in an undisciplined manner among you, nor did we eat anyone's bread without paying for it, but with labor and hardship we kept working night and day so that we would not be a burden to any of you; not because we do not have the right to this, but in order to offer ourselves as a model for you, so that you would follow our example. (2 Thessalonians 3:7-9)

> Let him who steals steal no longer, but rather let him labor, performing with his own hands what is good, in order that he may have something to share with him who has need. (Ephesians 4:28)

> Whatever you do, do your work heartily, as for the Lord rather than for men; knowing that from the Lord you will receive the reward of the inheritance. It is the Lord Christ whom you serve. (Colossians 3:23-24)

In 1964, President Johnson launched what would be called a "War on Poverty," largely using government as the tool to redistribute and disperse the nation's wealth. As a result, the welfare system created under Roosevelt in the thirties was greatly expanded, and this has helped create a different kind of poverty by stripping many people of the God-given dignity that's found in work.

It's true that even the "poor" are often overweight and have luxuries never dreamed of in the third world. In a "physical" sense, many there aren't poor at all. But the mentality of entitlement and of debilitating dependency is now even a greater "spiritual" poverty to overcome.

Governmental redistribution of wealth seems to impoverish the very people it wants to help. Yet the church continues to make the mistake our government made.

More than $500,000,000,000 in government aid has poured into Africa over the last fifty years, I recently read; yet the same article states that Africa is worse off economically than it was in 1949. Governmental redistribution of wealth seems to impoverish the very people it wants to help. Yet the church continues to make the mistake our government made. Money spent on giving things to the poor isn't nearly as well spent as money that empowers a couple to take care of themselves and their household. This is where the church must differ radically from the government. We must remember to keep intact that dignity given every human who was created in the image of God—dignity of personhood and dignity of work. Work is one way we were created in His image.

I was talking to a doctor just a few days ago about how she distributed food during a time of great famine in Uganda. She had jobs for everyone who was able—either to help with the distribution or to help start projects that would help prevent the next famine.

The people kept their dignity even in the most trying of times. No one complained for having to work. They thanked her for giving them a job to do. On the other hand, I've been told of government programs in poor countries that outright forbid making the needy work, and others that simply don't have them work because it requires more energy and thought on the part of the givers—but this, of course, sows the seeds of dependency while stripping people of their dignity. Certainly, those who are too sick to work need to be nurtured, cared for, and brought back to health. But when they're healthy, work is a good thing, and it's exactly what they need.

The Bible is quite clear on this matter:

> If anyone is not willing to work, then he is not to eat, either. For we hear that some among you are leading an undisciplined life, doing no work at all, but acting like busybodies. Now such persons we command and exhort in the Lord Jesus Christ to work in quiet fashion and eat their own bread. (2 Thessalonians 3:10-12)

We need to teach people the value of work, and empower them to eat of their own bread.

Ending poverty in this world isn't about redistributing our mounds of stuff and piles of money. It's about living more simply ourselves and using our money and our time to create jobs that allow people to function with the dignity of one created in God's image.

GIVING WISELY?

There's nothing inherently wrong with giving a few bucks to the man on the street with the sign "will work for food." But there's something far better: Actually getting this man back on his feet and off to work. It's so much easier to hand him a buck out the window. Who knows whether he *won't* work or *can't* work—because of mental or physical illness or a host of other reasons? It takes time, money, and work to actually provide work. But to provide work and to give the support the person needs to get back on his feet—that's the best use of our money; and there are many in the world dying to have such a chance.

There's nothing inherently wrong with giving a few bucks to the man on the street with the sign "will work for food." But there's something far better: Actually getting this man back on his feet and off to work.

These are places and people to whom our church and personal dollars should be flowing. If they're not, we're missing out on the very heart of God.

Part II:
RAISE

—

The Four Foundational Principles of True Generosity

Chapter Six

The Foundational Big Four

"A house with no foundation can be built twice
as fast, but cannot stand even half as long."

NOT A CHINESE PROVERB—BUT SHOULD HAVE BEEN.

"The rain came down, the rivers swelled, and
the winds raged and beat against that house
built on the sand, and it came crashing down."

JESUS

One lesson that has been painfully learned here in America is that money alone solves very few problems. In fact, in the case of such programs as welfare, it can create more serious problems and create a greater poverty than what it seeks to solve.

The church and individual believers, in our desire to give generously and to bless Christian workers from other cultures, and to bless those with great physical need in poor countries, can create the same problems we've seen created through welfare—both dependency and corruption. There's a good way to give that strengthens and empowers—and there's also a way to give that ultimately weakens and destroys.

Here's an introduction to some biblical principles that we must learn to employ when giving, particularly when giving cross-culturally.

Relationship First

A working and viable relationship is the foundation for wise giving.

It's interesting to note that when the apostle Paul went into Thessalonica, he worked "night and day" so as not to be a burden on anyone (2 Thessalonians 3:7-9). Before he had established a relationship with them, not only did he not ask for money, but he tended to flat out refuse it. It's clear that he believed that money too early in the relationship could cause distrust.

In the book of Acts, the earliest giving was done in the context of relationship; those who *had* gave to the ones they knew who *had not*.

Ask yourself: Is my relationship with the one I'm giving to one of mutual trust and respect, or superficially based on a well-presented speech or emotional appeal?

Accountability

There must be accountability.

The apostle Paul made sure this was in place. In 1 Corinthians 16:1-4 and again in 2 Corinthians 8:18-21, Paul puts systems of accountability into place for the administering of special offerings and gifts. He puts himself in a very accountable situation. If Paul believed *he* needed accountability, should we conclude anyone else is above such a need?

To give to an individual rather than through a financially accountable organization is not a sound practice and has led to the ruin of many believers.

Ask yourself: Who's responsible for setting the salary of the person I'm giving to, and who's making sure that what's given is spent for the purpose it was given?

Indigenous Sustainability

Our giving shouldn't create dependency, and it should work toward developing full indigenous sustainability.

Scripture teaches that those who receive teaching are to support those who teach them. How does this happen if all the needs are met by outsiders? And if the program cannot ultimately function in a given culture without outside help, how is it appropriate to the people? How can it grow to disciple the whole clan, tribe, and nation? Continuing a program or ministry only if it receives outside help is creating dependency, which cripples the receivers and weakens the church. Why should locals give to a pastor or ministry that's fully funded? Sadly we inadvertently teach locals not to give. Is that what we wish to do?

Ask yourself: Will the project I give to require ongoing and continual foreign funds to keep it alive, or are these funds seeding a plant that can be eventually watered and grown by locals?

Equity

The financial gift should not create economic inequities in the place it is given. Often pastors receiving western funds live at a standard high above those around him.

Since our economy is so different from those of the third world, it can be easy for us to underestimate the value of an American dollar overseas. Five dollars a week seems like a few cups of coffee for the average American, yet it can make a huge difference in the standard of living in the third world. When we give directly to national workers, we have to examine how even a small amount of financial support may set them apart from those whom they're called to serve. A salary of $500 a month may sound like peanuts to

GIVING WISELY?

us, but it often elevates one's standard of living to ten times above the average pastor in a given country.

Paul, writing to the Corinthians concerning a collection to be given to Christians elsewhere, says this:

> At this present time your abundance being a supply for their need, so that their abundance also may become a supply for your need, that there may be equality; as it is written, "He who gathered much did not have too much, and he who gathered little had no lack." (2 Corinthians 8:14-15)

Ask yourself: Does the money I give allow this man to live at a standard high above the rest of those he seeks to serve? Does this money elevate one child high above his next door neighbor?

Find out how much someone with an equivalent education and responsibilities makes in this man's or woman's country, and give accordingly.

Now that we've outlined these "RAISE" biblical principles (*R*elationship, *A*ccountability, *I*ndigenous *S*ustainability, and *E*quity)—let's examine each one in turn to understand how they can inform our giving and free us to use our money wisely, fulfilling the kingdom benefit we intend.

Paul and the RAISE Principles

I've spent twelve years overseas watching the effects that western money has had on Christians receiving it. I've now spent four more years in a position of overseeing the giving away of close to a million dollars a year. Firsthand, I've seen churches ruined by western wealth that was generously but unwisely dumped upon them. Stories come across my desk almost weekly about this abuse.

The Foundational Big Four

I've wrestled for years to come up with some principles that could help guide people to give wisely and constructively rather than in a way that hurts the one it was intended to help.

> *Firsthand, I have seen churches ruined by western wealth that was generously but unwisely dumped on them.*

Then a crisis of sorts came up here in Portland. A man was taking advantage of numerous groups who were all well-intentioned and extremely generous. A number of us felt the need to help educate these groups so they could see the negative cost of giving to this man. We called a meeting. We were five missionaries, one with a doctorate who's a professor in missiology, and we'd spent a cumulative time of close to eighty years overseas. Out of this meeting came four guiding principles for giving wisely that we all agreed upon.

These four principles had taken me twelve years to just begin to understand; then 80 years of accumulated experience and four hours of meetings. But these same

> *These same principles, I was astonished to find, were all right there staring up at us from the pages of Acts.*

principles, I was astonished to find, were all right there staring up at us from the pages of Acts. Paul already knew them all. He practiced and applied them. He didn't learn them through observation and trial and error like I had. He started out with them. I was amazed. The principles were under my nose to begin with. The Bible proved itself to me once again.

This discovery led me to the conclusion that our relationship to the Bible has some serious problems. Two, to be exact: (1) I don't read it enough. (2) I don't apply its principles like I should. If we could get back to what's modeled and taught in the New Testament,

GIVING WISELY?

we would do well. Our money could be more fully used to benefit the cause of the gospel, and be so much less likely to harm it.

Relationship and Accountability

In Acts 20, there's a list of men with names that are hard to read, from places with names that are even harder to read—the men who were accompanying the apostle Paul: Sopater of Berea, the son of Pyrrhus, Aristarchus and Secumdus of the Thessalonians, Gaius of Derbe, and Timothy, and Tychicus and Trophimus of Asia.

We can stumble across these names and get onto the "meat" in the passage, failing to realize we've just missed the main course. These were men from all the churches Paul had been working with. So why were they with Paul?

The churches around the region had taken an offering for the poor and the victims of the drought that was plaguing the people in and around Jerusalem. But Paul refused to take the money himself. Each church sent a man whom they trusted to accompany their offering back to Jerusalem. Why? *An offering detached from relationship does not fully affect the receiver, nor does it fully touch the giver.*

> *An offering detached from relationship does not fully affect the receiver, nor does it fully touch the giver.*

Option 1: Send a lump of money with someone you won't see again, and the offering is over.

Option 2: Send it with someone who will help administer it, keep it safe, watch God work, then come back and share the many-faceted effect it had, and the offering just keeps on giving.

See it also from this perspective:

Option 1: Receive a lump of money and spend it, and the offering is over.

Option 2: Receive the offering *and* the giver of the offering into your home, hear what God is doing as far away as the other side of the sea in the lives of Gentiles and Jews a like, get to share what God is doing in Jerusalem, encourage each other in Christ even though you're from entirely different cultures—and the gift keeps giving. It stays alive.

Send a lump of cash with only Paul the apostle, while the ship sinks and the money is lost but Paul escapes—or else a band of robbers steals the money from him—and Paul's reputation is forever ruined. Not a good option.

Better: Send the cash with your best and most trustworthy man on a missionary journey with a group of similar guys from churches all over, plus the most radical missionary of all times, all holding each other accountable continually, assuring the delivery of the gift, fellowshipping with believers from other cultures and places, seeing God work in radical ways, and returning home a changed man, and sharing with everyone in church.

"But," comes an objection I've heard, "it costs extra money to send a man that whole way. It all could have been given to the poor."

True, the poor would have had a few extra bucks (provided it hadn't been stolen along the way). But they would have lost much of the real value. And that which would have been of greatest value to the churches who gave would have been completely lost as well.

Paul, executing the Holy Spirit's plan, was a genius. Yet often the church and individuals today simply cut a check—and so ends the gift. To quote the apostle James, "Brothers, it ought not be this way."

Indigenous Sustainability and Equity

What's most surprising and at greatest contrast to the modern missions methods of our time was the quickness with which Paul got into an area and then quickly back out again. He would plant the local church, set up leadership, and hand it over ASAP to the locals. They had no paid pastor, no paid staff, no building, and no leadership with formal theological training.

He would plant the local church, set up leadership, and hand it over ASAP to the locals. They had no paid pastor, no paid staff, no building, and no leadership with formal theological training.

But still he handed it over to them. They had to figure the rest out.

Paul did not tell them to send out advertisements or set up a search committee so they could find a great speaker or a senior pastor from some far-off place. No, they had the Holy Spirit, and men in their midst could rise to the occasion. In the power of the Holy Spirit, it wasn't necessary for some full-time worker to come save them—they could do the work on their own. A bit of contrast from today.

Never did Paul set up some system where they could get income from other, wealthier churches. He believed that either the local body had what it needed, or God could soon provide it from within.

Never did Paul set up some system where they could get income from other, wealthier churches.

He set up indigenously sustainable churches, and he did this from the very beginning.

Paul himself would often refuse to take money from the local church so they would know beyond a doubt that it wasn't money

The Foundational Big Four

that motivated him. He reminded churches of this later on when accusations came against him. He would have had a weak defense had he not stayed way above reproach. He didn't put money into the mix at all until after he left, and then wrote that the laborer (teacher) is worthy of his wages, and an elder who teaches is worthy of double honor (probably meaning pay for his time given). Paul indicated that it was good to pay folks who are putting in the time, but it wasn't even necessarily full time. And nowhere in Scripture do we see the model we've exported around the world of a single full-time pastor doing all the teaching and preaching and ministry.

The "one man does all" model of ministry is neither prescribed nor even seen in Scripture. We see a plurality of leadership, most who do it part time without pay, and a few—if the local church should see someone with a gifting and who's putting in many hours to the task of teaching—with pay.

> *It wasn't up to a single pastor to make them sink or swim. It was up to the local body—the whole body working together.*

Paul left this up to the local church to decide. The locals had been given the authority to govern and lead themselves in the power of the Holy Spirit. They were not dependent on outside funds. They were quickly—very quickly—given ownership. It wasn't up to a single pastor to make them sink or swim. It was up to the local body—the whole body working together.

Chapter Seven

RAISE: Relationship First

The Only Way Everyone Wins

We have profoundly forgotten everywhere
that Cash-payment is not the sole relation of
human beings.
THOMAS CARLYLE

Having so fond an affection for you, we were
well-pleased to impart to you not only the
gospel of God but also our own lives, because
you had become very dear to us. For you
recall, brethren, our labor and hardship, how
working night and day so as not to be a
burden to any of you, we proclaimed to you
the gospel of God.
PAUL THE APOSTLE

Many of us are moved to give to a particular person or ministry because of an emotional tug at our hearts. We hear a powerful testimony and see the huge need, and we give in complete confidence that our money will be used wisely. God has given us emotions, and He uses them to move our hearts and to give us a heart like His.

But wise and healthy giving doesn't take place at this level alone. The healthiest giving is best done at a relational level, not merely the emotional level.

Is it better to buy a used car from a trustworthy family friend who you know to be a reliable mechanic, or to listen to a smooth sales pitch and buy from an unknown used car salesman in a big city far from home? So often in the church community our giving follows the emotional appeal rather than the reality of a trustworthy and open relationship.

> Is it better to buy a used car from a trustworthy family friend who you know to be a reliable mechanic, or to listen to a smooth sales pitch and buy from an unknown used car salesman in a big city far from home?

It's a good thing to give to a relief organization to help the poor because you saw a need on an effective TV commercial, but it's even better to give to a relief organization that you have personal connection to and a relationship with. Perhaps there's a trusted and well-respected former staff member from your church who's now working in some needy area with a relief organization, and you can read his words, believe his reports, and both hear and see the needs he has around him. Giving through this organization to a specific area where you know your friend will use your money with the utmost integrity is vastly superior to the response we have to a television commercial.

When there's a real working relationship between the one giving and the one receiving, there's a maximum benefit for both sides. Four critical things are achieved in relationships that form a healthy foundation for financial giving.

1. There's opportunity for *reciprocity*, where those in the relationship are able to give and receive in different ways—praying for one another, teaching each other, serving each other.

2. There's a natural, built-in *accountability*.

GIVING WISELY?

3.   There's also — in a good relationship — a natural *transparency* and blunt honesty that doesn't exist in a mere financial transaction.

4.   There's also a line of *open communication* that can clear up and prevent many misunderstandings.

Where there's no relationship, all these elements that are critical for the long-term health of a person or ministry are lost.

Our church got involved in a certain ministry in England because the charismatic leader with a powerful testimony convinced us God was doing great things through this ministry. Fortunately, instead of getting involved

Where there is no relationship, all these elements that are critical for the long-term health of a person or ministry are lost.

financially right off the bat, we sent a summer team to establish the relationship. At first we liked what we saw, but the team had a couple of reservations about the leader himself — namely that he was always traveling around the world raising money instead of being at home with his ministry in his church. We became good friends with several folks who worked under the leader and soon saw that many were quitting because of the leader's mishandling of funds. He had two homes, drove a very nice car and was living at a standard no one in his church could come close to. We knew then that we were not to get further involved with this ministry.

The reason this man was able to live so much in luxury is because churches would respond financially to his charismatic and emotional appeals. His stories could grip the heart of anyone inducing many to give — feeding his corruption.

If these churches would have first responded relationally instead of with their checkbooks, this pastor likely would have never been empowered to live such an extravagant lifestyle, bringing shame to the name of Christ.

If these churches would first respond relationally instead of with their checkbook, this likely would have never happened

Churches need to learn to respond in working relationships first and then let our money follow these proven and trust-filled relationships.

It's a great thing to know that the money you're investing is going to trustworthy people ministering in effective and Christ-like ways, and this can really only be known through working relationships.

Relationship also guarantees a level of involvement that includes ongoing concern, pastoral care, and prayer for projects and people. The relationship isn't merely financial but multifaceted, healthy, and dynamic.

There was once a generous father. He had no time for his son, but he had money. His son would approach him with his latest need, all justified by marvelous stories. The father, being deeply moved, would reach into his pocket and give his son cash. Such a loving father! Whenever his son had any need, it was always responded to with quick cash. There was never a relationship—but boy, was there *money!*

No need to end this story. You know where the boy ends up, and it isn't good. Yet we Christians in the West often do the same thing. Because a relationship is hard—it takes time, work, and energy—we instead take an offering, write a check, and send it to our "son" overseas.

Just as relationship must precede financial gifts in the context of a family, so too in the body of Christ.

In the same way that there's a great peace and certainty in taking your car to a mechanic who happens to be your close friend, so there's the same peace in giving to a person or ministry that you're involved with in an ongoing relationship. As a general principle,

As a general principle, it's far better for money to follow a good relationship than to start with money and then try to develop a relationship.

it's far better for money to follow a good relationship than to start with money and then try to develop a relationship. And the least desirable of all? That money is given completely apart from any real relationship.

Support of Missionaries—Sending and Not Merely Supporting

> How then will they call on Him in whom they have not believed? How will they believe in Him whom they have not heard? And how will they hear without a preacher? How will they preach unless they are sent? (Romans 10:14-15)

> As the Father has sent me, so send I you. (Jesus)

Every church needs to send out its own people who have heard the message of Jesus to those who have not.

The closer the relationship, the more meaningful the giving. Many churches make the mistake of supporting missionaries they know little about, and have virtually no relationship with. The church loses in this weak relationship and

Many churches make the mistake of supporting missionaries they know little of, and have virtually no relationship with.

RAISE Relationship First

so does the missionary.

The Church's Role

A close friend of mine, on hearing that my family was headed to East Asia to work with university students, got really excited. "My church might support you guys. It's a great missions church. We support over fifty missionaries."

I later found out that his church had only about 150 members.

God bless the good intentions of this small church. They have a heart for the world, and show it by taking on as many missionaries as possible. This is the model of many churches out there. The more faces up on that missionary board—the more red dots on the map marking the families they support financially around the world— the better.

But is there something better?

Yes, I think so. And it's all about depth in relationship, not merely numbers who receive checks.

Let's suppose a church has a budget of $40,000 a year to support missionaries around the world. Contrast these two models for how to use those funds:

Traditional supporting approach: Support fifty missionaries anywhere from $50 to $100 a month each. If someone asks for support, and his or her story is compelling—give. These people may be a friend of an elder or a cousin of the pastor, but the fact is, the church as a whole doesn't really know any of them. They may have an opportunity to come and speak once every six to eight years for twenty minutes after a Sunday night service or at a special meeting during the week, but since they have no real relationship with the whole body of the church, few in the church will feel a sense of ownership. The twenty-five people or so who came to that one meeting and heard the missionaries are motivated to pray for a year or so, but again, since there was no depth of relationship, in time they're forgotten and confused with the other fifty missionaries that are supported by the church. On the other hand, these missionaries are supported by some twenty to twenty-five churches of this kind and cannot—without killing themselves—possibly visit all of these churches. Since they have no real relationship with the church, they feel no sense of obligation to spend much time there when home— further ensuring that a real relationship will never grow between this faithful giving church and the faithfully receiving missionary. This relationship has been effectively reduced to a small financial transaction once a month with no one benefiting like they should from the relationship.

Sending approach: This is the more biblical model—to send out one of your own, rather than simply giving money to someone from outside. A $40,000 budget might then be used to support two or three missionary families from your own church body, rather than fifty from all over. The benefits to such an approach are huge, and it's in no way less spiritual just because the number of pictures on the missionary wall has been reduced.

Here are the advantages:

1. Sending your own people — those who have grown up and served in your church — means they're known by you and you're known by them. Values and principles are shared. People in the congregation will pray so much more for someone they've known for some time.

2. When they're home, they don't have to run around frantically, because the vast majority of their support

base is right here at home. By supporting them significantly, you allow them to come home when they're on furlough rather than running to twenty-five churches that don't know them from Adam trying desperately to gain support. Believe it or not, most missionaries get so exhausted on their furlough (which should be a time of rest) that they can't wait to get back on the field to take a break. A significant level of support means they'll be able to spend a significant amount of time at the supporting church when home. This again, allows the relationship to grow.

> *People in the congregations will pray so much more for someone they've known for some time.*

An example: Our church supports our missionaries at between twenty-five and fifty percent of their total support, and we then require them to be home at our church that percentage of their time when they're on furlough. Actually, we have them add in that percentage of support they get from individuals in our church. If it comes to a total of, let's say, 70 percent, then they must spend 70 percent of their furlough time here. Being told to stay in one place, and not having to fret about running to raise support, is a missionary's dream come true.

3. Since there's relationship, the church at home seeks to meet other needs. Short-term teams can be sent to empower the ministry of the missionaries. There are usually pastoral visits. Letters home become a big deal, because these missionaries aren't someone "out there" — they're part of this church.

All these things continue to add to the strength of this relationship.

The Family's and Individual's Role

Some have asked me why our church doesn't support our missionaries 100 percent, instead of only 25 to 50 percent. It all has to do with relationship. Missionaries need individuals and families to be a part of what they're doing. This fosters another kind of win/win relationship.

At this very moment my brother, doing missionary work in Central Asia, has some American visitors doing ministry with him. This doctor started supporting my brother financially, and then his family began praying. They got so involved in my brother's life that they've now become more than just supporters. He goes with his family to lecture in the medical universities. This not only gives this doctor a chance to share Jesus, but it gives my brother people to work with, plus great standing in the government's eyes for providing such a skilled American surgeon lecturer.

This is just one story of how individuals and families have been changed when they adopt a missionary family by financially supporting them. Some churches support their missionaries 100 percent, but I've seen relationships reduced by such a policy. Those who receive 100 percent support from their denomination and church don't have nearly the number of individuals and families really tracking with them and praying for them back home. And whenever relationship is reduced, the healthy impact of giving is also reduced.

If the church stops sending our own, and instead sends our money to far-off countries to support those we don't know, the mission movement in this country will die in this generation.

It's my desire that every Christian family get to know a missionary family, then begin to give in the context of that relationship. In the health of this giving relationship, I've seen many lives challenged and changed. It's truly one of the best ways to invest.

GIVING WISELY?

We need to send our own. We need to send our best. If the church stops sending our own, and instead sends our money to far-off countries to support those we don't know, the mission movement in this country will die in this generation. It's our relationship with these people that keeps the flame of the Great Commission burning.

I asked a missionary in Africa to read over this manuscript for suggestions, and this is the chapter he wanted to emphasize. Listen to his words:

> My suggestion: We need more foreign personnel "on the field," but they shouldn't be loaded! That is — they need enough money to get them there and keep them alive, but they should not be supporting their ministry with their own funds. So, while the U.S. church is good at giving money, much of the problem is that money giving has outstripped people-giving. Is it not time to take the emphasis from sending money to sending people?

There's no greater endeavor for a church than to send out our own people to the ends of the earth to proclaim and live the gospel.

There's no more satisfying way to give than to send those you know and want God to use greatly.

And there's no more satisfying way for an individual to give than to send those you know and want God to use greatly.

God sent his Son. Jesus sent his disciples. The church sent out the apostles. We need to be sending our own. It's biblical through and through.

Chapter Eight

RAISE: Accountability
Without Which We Destroy Even the Best of Men

Do not value money for any more nor any less
than its worth; it is a good servant but a bad
master.
ALEXANDRE DUMAS

No one can serve two masters. Either he will
hate the one and love the other, or he will be
devoted to the one and despise the other. You
cannot serve both God and Money.

JESUS

For the love of money is a root of all kinds
of evil. Some people, in their lust for money,
have strayed from the faith and pierced
themselves with many griefs.

PAUL THE APOSTLE

When it comes to accountability, consider the following
Scripture passages and Paul's plea that we leave no ground
for anyone to discredit God's work:

> Now concerning the collection for the saints,
> as I directed the churches of Galatia, so do you
> also.

> On the first day of every week each one of you is to put aside and save, as he may prosper, so that no collections be made when I come. When I arrive, whomever you may approve, I will send them with letters to carry your gift to Jerusalem; and if it is fitting for me to go also, they will go with me. (1 Corinthians 16:1-4)

> We have sent along with him the brother whose fame in the things of the gospel has spread through all the churches; and not only this, but he has also been appointed by the churches to travel with us in this gracious work, which is being administered by us for the glory of the Lord Himself, and to show our readiness, taking precaution so that no one will discredit us in our administration of this generous gift; for we have regard for what is honorable, not only in the sight of the Lord, but also in the sight of men. (2 Corinthians 8:18-21)

Recently, a woman contacted me regarding an opportunity to support a national worker directly. This meant of course there would be no administrative accountability. The following is my response, warning her of the dangers of such an arrangement. (The names and places have been changed and details of events have been altered.)

> Dear Carrie,
> Thank you so much for your call and for contacting us regarding your Nepalese friend. She sounds like a true gem. What a privilege you have had to be able to be involved in her life.
> Whenever someone elects to support a national directly, there are a number of things that must be considered. Having lived overseas for the last ten years, I have seen firsthand and have heard of numerous other difficulties that arise when doing so.

In responding to your request, I would like to share a scenario with you that is based on my observations and experience. The following is very typical of what I have seen time and again.

Ben was from a needy country and more than anything wanted to see his people reached with the gospel. He came to the United States, attended seminary, and then joined an organization to help him do just that. Ben became frustrated with the organization because they did not always agree with him and not all the money that he had raised went to his ministry. He began to request that his donors send the money directly to him so that it would not get docked the seven percent administrative fee and he could use all of the Lord's money for his vision to build a Bible School. He spoke at a church and mentioned that $10,000 was needed to build the new Bible School. The church caught the vision and gave him the $10,000.

As he got back to his country, he found that his child was extremely sick and needed to be hospitalized. He was fearful of his child dying, yet did not have the money to take him to the best hospital that he knew was needed to save him. "But wait," he thought, "God had just provided $10,000."

He reasoned that those people back in America loved him and his family, and certainly they would understand this predicament. So he spent $2,000 on his son and $8,000 on the school.

As he got back to his country, he found that his child was extremely sick and needed to be hospitalized.

The next project he was involved in cost $20,000. He raised the money in the United States, and when he got into his project, his daughter came home with the bad news that she had lost her college scholarship midway through her junior year.

They did not have the $2,000 to help her finish. Again — the Lord had provided. He could spend $2,000 on her education and use the remaining $18,000 to finish his project adequately.

The next time he went to the United States to raise money, he had in mind his three other children who would soon be entering the university. They could do so much more for Jesus with the education, and all he had to do was add a few extra dollars to each project.

Soon, this man with a heart and passion for God had become one who saw money as a means of buying everything he wanted. Americans had nice homes — they wouldn't care if he built himself a nice one with the leftover money.

Now if this were an isolated incident, that would be one thing. But I have seen it happen over and over again whenever a national is supported directly rather than through a trustworthy organization.

> Soon, this man with a heart and passion for God had become one who saw money as a means of buying everything he wanted.

My family and I have just returned to the United States from Asia. While we were there, a lovely Christian family started an orphanage. Later it was discovered that they had used foreign funds designated to build the orphanage to build themselves a nice home.

One third world brother even left a reputable, fiscally responsible organization to work with another, with no overhead and seemingly no accountability, so that he could have control and access to all the money.

Our church gave to this organization, only to realize that it was the same as giving directly to him and not holding him fiscally responsible. We are in the process of trying to figure out if this money was spent the way it should have been.

I am not saying that your friend is going to do this or has this in mind — but I am afraid we are setting a trap for her to fall into by not making sure she is held fiscally responsible. The only way to make sure there is no trap is to have her work under the accountability of a trustworthy and known organization.

I have seen too many wonderful brothers and sisters in third world countries corrupted by money that we, well-intentioned Americans, give to them when we hear of a need. We think, "Wow, what a testimony! Certainly they will be responsible with my money." But the truth is that they have never even had to learn what fiscal responsibility is — for they have never had any money to speak of. I am not righteous enough to say that if I were put in that circumstance, I would not totally be overtaken by the money — and ultimately, the enemy. This is not just the third world — I've seen it happen here in the United States to good men. The temptation can be overpowering.

As a church, we have established the policy of not supporting nationals directly. We do support some nationals, but always through an organization that has the highest reputation for fiscal responsibility. We have learned this the hard way.

This is not just the third world — I've seen it happen here in the United States to good men. The temptation can be overpowering.

I hope you see that I am in no way saying your friend's motives are impure, but that we as Americans need to do all we can to make sure we are not setting a trap for them, for we want their motives to stay pure.

Hebrews 13:5 says, "Make sure that your character is free from the love of money, being content with what you have; for He Himself has said, 'I will never desert you, nor will I ever forsake you.'"

We need to be generous and give much to the underdeveloped places in this world. We have so very much here in America. But we need to do all we can to not ruin a brother or sister in the process. My recommendation is to find a ministry managed by a trustworthy, fiscally responsible organization in your friend's country to oversee the dispensing of money and track the use of funds.

If you have any questions, please don't hesitate to call.

Jonathan

Imagine the employees of a company begging their boss not to hire an accountant. "It will leave more profits for us," they argue. "With those profits we can build the company faster and it can become stronger faster."

Such thinking is preposterous. What kind of monster might emerge from such slime?

> *Imagine the employees of a company begging their boss not to hire an accountant. "It will leave more profits for us," they argue.*

It's the same situation when someone asks you to avoid the overhead costs of an organization to support him or her directly. They're asking for the same problems. This is a problem you don't want to give them. Gifts are sometimes fine if they come once a year at Christmas, but they should never come as regular support.

I've learned to invite financial accountability for myself. In dealing with the money that passes through my office I need to have people asking the hard questions. I've told the elders of the church to ask these hard questions: "Don't think you might offend me by a question you have. If I get offended, it's time to start distrusting me. If I ask impatiently, 'Don't you trust me?' Then by all means, please don't."

I know my own tendency to be deceived. The power of money can lead us down dark roads. I, for one, don't want to go there. And I, for one, don't want to send a dear brother or sister in Christ down such a road either. Dumping money on someone without accountability is a sure way to make your brother stumble. And the Bible does teach us this one thing: We are our brother's keeper.

These words of Boris Yeltsin in 1994 are and have always been true:

> Money, big money (which is actually a relative concept) is always, under any circumstances, a seduction, a test of morals, a temptation to sin.

RAISE Accountability

Chapter Nine

RA_ISE_: Indigenous Sustainability
Getting Over the Maternal Instinct

"Built to Last"
FORD MOTOR COMPANY

The things which you have heard from me in
the presence of many witnesses, entrust these
to faithful men who will be able to teach others
also.

PAUL THE APOSTLE

Sometimes we think a church in a poor country needs our money, but in actuality this isn't the case. Every believer in every culture must learn to give, and as soon as someone from the outside starts giving, the felt need for the local congregation to give immediately stops.

When China closed its doors to the West in 1949, there was no longer any foreign funding of the church. It was in this extremely poor China that the church grew like wildfire.

Our financial underwriting of a church or its pastor takes away the local ownership and local accountability. Our money is better spent training the locals to be self-sufficient.

> *Our financial underwriting of a church or its pastor takes away the local ownership and the local accountability.*

We in the United States, or other extremely wealthy countries, often arrogantly presume we'll always be wealthy and we'll be able indefinitely to financially underwrite certain projects. The truth is that our economy could crash tomorrow. And in that case, only the extent to which we helped the work become indigenous will matter. Only the indigenous part will continue in our absence.

Western missionaries and NGOs —nongovernmental organizations formed to help the poor - often have to pull out when there's political tension or turmoil, and often have had to flee in the face of war. With our own future involvement at question in any given country, it's only cultural presumption and perhaps even arrogance that would dare keep others dependent on our generosity, and it's such arrogance that keeps many organizations from working toward indigenous sustainability.

Certainly, works like Bible translation, and saving those dying from starvation, and even providing for the widows and orphans in some impoverished countries, are not considered to be sustainable. But even in these, whenever we can give in ways that encourage local sustainability, it's best for everyone. It's always good to ask how you might give in a way that this could become sustainable.

I recently met with a dear friend whom I've been with in a mentoring relationship. He was orphaned during the war in Liberia. All foreigners fled the country for their lives, and for the next ten years life was a living hell. As a child, my friend Kerkula saw his friends shot while walking right beside him. He had to step over countless dead bodies in the streets, and in her effort to save her eight children from starvation, his mom starved herself and succumbed to illness and death. Relatives split the children up but couldn't even take care of their own children. Eventually an orphanage took them in. Later, when the war died down for a time, a family in the U.S adopted Kerkula and his siblings. I asked him how this local orphanage that took him in was funded.

It was run and funded entirely by the locals. There was no other choice. All the foreigners had fled along with their money.

The orphanages that were funded and run by outsiders did the people little or no good when the outsiders had to flee. Those that relied on the local believers and churches still managed to function and save lives when the foreign money dried up.

> *It was run and funded entirely by the locals. There was no other choice. All the foreigners had fled along with their money.*

God calls the local church—even in these countries that are poor by our standards—to take care of the widows and orphans.

We can go in with our grand plans to build an amazing orphan facility and completely fund it with tourist dollars, but there's a serious problem. What happens when there's a war and the locals haven't been taught and trained to take care of their own? What happens to the 20,000 orphans who have been removed from their culture and can no longer fit back in? Such plans are ultimately doomed to fail—and it's better that they fail earlier rather than later.

Once, when walking the streets with a Muslim friend of mine, I made a comment about the beggars, saying that it must be hard for them to be out of work.

"They're not out of work," he replied. "That's their job. Their job is to beg."

"What do you mean?" I asked.

"The Koran says we must give alms to the beggars. That's part of the way we earn heaven. Therefore we need beggars so we can give

GIVING WISELY?

alms to them. Their job as beggar is just as important as my job as a dentist."

Imagine that: Become a beggar, and help a guy get to heaven.

In such a culture, there's no reason to really help the guy get back on his feet again, for he exists for the purpose of receiving alms.

As believers in Jesus, we're called to something different. We're *Imagine that: Become a beggar, and help a guy get to heaven.* called to make every effort to make a real and lasting difference. We don't merely give because it helps us work our way to heaven. We want to have a heart like Jesus — a heart of compassion — a heart that desires to make a lasting and even eternal difference. We won't express our compassion perfectly, but this must be our goal.

We need to consider how our dollars can train and empower the locals to do the work they're called to. They're the ones who understand their own culture and know how to raise people up in it. Our dollars can assist, start, and train—but we must work toward making it indigenously sustainable. *We won't express our compassion perfectly, but our goal must be to make a lasting and eternal difference.*
Then when it becomes sustainable, we can move on to train others to do the same and our dollar touches more lives than we could have ever imagined.

Chopping Their Legs Out from Under Them

Money often costs too much. (Ralph Emerson)

There is a road that seems right to a man, but in the end it leads to death. (Hebrew Proverb)

My father often tells a story that one of his seminary professors told to him years ago: Charles had gone to Africa to visit some missionary friends. He stayed with the small group of missionaries living on a mission compound with hopes to encourage them. Near the end of his stay, he invited all the missionaries there to go into the local town with him so he could treat them to a sit down restaurant dinner. The group was delighted, except — they informed him — not all could go. Someone would have to stay behind to watch the compound.

"Well, can't you get a national to watch after the house and the stuff?" Charles inquired.

"It's not so easy as that," the compound leader replied. "We really don't have any one we can trust. The locals aren't that trustworthy."

"Surely, there's one person you could trust to take care of the place while we're gone just a few hours?" Charles pushed.

"Not really. We've tried it before and have always been sorry. They're really quite dishonest, and something will end up broken or stolen. Even if they're honest, one of their family members will come in and make trouble."

"So, there's nobody? Not one local who can watch the mission while we're away?"

"No one. We'll just leave one of us behind."

So they left one behind and headed in for a night on the town. Charles felt terrible for having to leave someone out. And even more, he could hardly believe there was no one — not even one national — who could be trusted. This fact led him to ask another question later that evening.

"So how long has this mission been here in this location?" he asked the head of the mission.

"One hundred years."

What had they really accomplished in those hundred years?

The following letter was written to a mission agency that believed it expedient to hire and support national pastors and church workers with foreign funds. This begs the question: What will be the future ramifications? My letter is perhaps a bit strong, but this philosophy is so prevalent I felt the emotion and need to be strong.

> Dear Joseph,
>
> It's the stated goal of most mission agencies to raise up and train locals, and to ultimately have the indigenous people run the ministry by themselves. If this isn't the stated goal, then something's wrong. But there are different and varied means to this end. Some of the most common methods end up short-circuiting the system, and the desired end is never achieved.
>
> Then the missionaries sit there wondering why the locals never take any initiative, when they themselves have unknowingly set up a system that insures that they never will. This is tragic, yet it's unavoidable when the wrong route is chosen. The problem is this: The wrong route often seems at first to be the easy and right one.
>
> When a new missionary arrives in a city where there are few, if any, believers, the first goal is to reach these folks for Christ, and the second is to disciple and raise up local leadership.

The wrong route often seems at first to be the easy and right one.

Raise Indigenous Sustainability

So when someone comes to Christ and is a promising leader, we fine-tune them in leadership and soon they're ready to go. We can hardly contain our excitement. This is what we've been living for. The only problem is this: This capable and trained person has to make a living and can only give a couple hours a night to ministry. "If only they could be full-time." Full-time means more ministry time, and this is better because it will speed things up.

Seems good. Makes sense. Why not?

Well, for one, this is clearly the exporting of a western style of ministry. This is the way we do it in the United States and so we figure it's best for them. This isn't necessarily a biblical model, yet it's our western default. But by thinking this is best and by getting them to become full-time in a culture where there's no such thing as a full-time ministry worker, we've just made the local leadership not at all "local" — but very foreign indeed.

> *So this local leader is perceived to be absolutely foreign by his own people, thus losing his credibility. In our desire to raise up locals quickly, we've failed to raise up anything local at all.*

Our means for funding full-time ministry are also very foreign. Since this is a completely unknown concept, the locals have no vision for it, and there aren't enough believers in the local community to support them. The foreign missionary must look outside the local community, and back to America, for the support for this national. So you have the national doing something very foreign, and doing it for a "foreign" paycheck.

"No wonder he spreads the gospel. Foreigners are paying him to do it. I would do it too for a nice paycheck." Oh, the times I've heard these words.

So this local leader is perceived to be absolutely foreign by his own people, thus losing his credibility. In our desire to raise up locals quickly, we've failed to raise up anything local at all.

Not only have we failed to do so, but we've just created a model for ministry that will be propagated for years and maybe decades to come.

Africa is the classic case in point. Church buildings were built with foreign money and they were built much better than the local homes. Pastors were paid with outside money. Since the work was started this way, the mentality that it should continue this way is so pervasive that it amazes me. Churches there often say, "We cannot do anything because we have no money." They've falsely learned that money is the answer to everything, and that a nice building (that they cannot afford) is necessary if meaningful ministry is to take place. Local initiative and giving is extremely stunted, for there's no reason for church members to give to the church. And why not? Because there's an outside source of funding.

China, on the other hand, is something quite different. After a hundred years of missionary work, the church was small and largely dependent upon the West and looking very western indeed. Then all the missionaries were kicked out. So full-time Christian workers — which had been the model — were for the most part, no more. The work — if it was to be done — had to be done by those who held down a normal job. Funding vanished as foreign money was cut off. China became miserably poor.

There was now no full-time pastor to be paid. The little money that was given each week went to meet needs. Church buildings were confiscated. How could they have church without the nice building that westerners had built them?

They moved into the homes.

So, no full-time staff? No building? No money? And oops I almost forgot — no academic institutions for formal theological training? These are the four things we in the West deem as most important, and yet it was in the absence of these things that arguably the greatest church growth in history has taken place. China's one million believers turned into forty million by the late 1980s and now perhaps to as many as 100 million.

Is the church there perfect? Far from it. All churches are imperfect. But it does look very much like the church that's described in the first century. And it's so much healthier than in the lands where people wait for a handout before they start ministering.

RAiSE Indigenous Sustainability

It's my opinion that when we take someone who's serving Christ two hours a day because of his love for Christ and people, and then give him foreign money to do it full-time, we're unintentionally cutting the legs out from under the local church. We set up a model for ministry that leads to paralysis, and we end up with a lame church holding out its hands and asking for alms from passers-by.

It's a sad indictment upon modern missionary methods when the country that kicks out foreigners and their funding is the one that goes wild with the gospel; and the continent that has always welcomed foreign funding sits with its hands out waiting for the paternal West to call the shots.

There's a significant move in Africa to make up for the wrongs that we as Westerners have perpetrated against them and to restore local initiative, and progress is being made by many missionaries. But as long as generous but uninformed and misguided westerners keep pouring the money into the wrong projects and pockets, this attitude will stay alive and well. It's really a shame if missionaries continue the same practices that led to such paralysis, especially in countries where the gospel is just arriving. It's my observation that today we're more often making this mistake in these unreached countries than not.

We must ask ourselves whether we really want to see an indigenous movement. Sure, we say we do; but it's not so easy when we see the locals taking things in a different direction, and we so easily step in and intervene. Even if we truly desire to teach them to do things in what we perceive is the right way, we may be actually teaching them to wait on our decision and direction at every turn. It's also extremely difficult for us wealthy Westerners to watch and wait on the locals when they're slow to give money to do ministry, and so again we step in. We may think that we're teaching them to give, and leading by example by our generous giving, but really we're teaching them that they need us and cannot really do it without us, and we're reinforcing their tendency to look to us for direction. After all, we're the hand that feeds them.

It's amazing to see how quickly Paul was in and then out of a given place—handing things over to the locals quickly and not paying them a cent to do the work.

The gospel spread like wildfire and lives were changed and the whole face of the Roman Empire was transformed. Did the churches he plant have struggles? Tons. But they did the job. They took initiative and did what Christ commanded.

Sorry if this seems a bit strong, but I am getting way too many stories across my desk confirming the realities I outlined above. Take care, Joseph.

Jonathan

My friend Ralph has served and trained Christian leaders in Russia for years—way before the Soviet era came to an end, until now. He told a group of us recently how money has affected the church there in profound ways:

The Soviet Union, under the communist leadership, prohibited tithing to the church. It was against the law. The government paid the salaries of the clergy and provided the money for the upkeep of whatever church facilities they allowed to remain open. This was an extremely shrewd way for the communist government to exercise its control over the church. Your preaching gets out of line —no paycheck. Too much evangelism and the heat at the church gets turned off. By being the sole donor of the church, they were the ones calling the shots and therefore prohibiting indigenous sustainability.

At the collapse of the Soviet Union, this flow of cash from the government dried up rather quickly. For the past seventy years of communism the church members had never learned to tithe and give to the church. It was now a pivotal time in the history of the church —they could now take the necessary steps to become indigenously sustainable by having their hand forced in respect to giving. But...

Enter a new Big Brother—the church from the West. When the communist government stopped paying pastors' salaries, we stepped in and supported them handsomely. More money poured in than ever before, causing the roots of dependency to grow even deeper.

The irony is this: The very technique the shrewd communist government used to control the church is the exact same that the western church uses. Both have the same effect. There's a huge disconnect between the leaders and their people. The leaders are owned by something outside the local church, and the local church can never become what it was intended to be.

I remember well the appeals for money for Russia from practically every Christian organization on the planet. At the same time I never heard talk of making the Russian church indigenously sustainable. What has been the impact of all this money on the church? Well, the funds have slowly been drying up from the West (as we give to other great causes), leaving the church with a mental hangover that it was somehow the money that did the ministry. And now that there's no money—the assumed resource for ministry —little ministry is therefore being done.

> *Well, the funds have slowly been drying up from the West (as we give to other great causes), leaving the church with a mental hangover that it was somehow the money that did the ministry.*

Of course, this isn't every church in Russia. But as Ralph explained, it's the prevalent attitude. He saw converts being bought from the local church or "poorer" organizations by another who had more western money. He also saw western churches come in and literally buy whole ministries: "We'll give your church (or ministry) X amount of dollars if you let us come in and run it—and pay you too, of course."

Ironically, Ralph said, it wasn't the nationals who said "no" to such offers, for this was what they've been taught for many years. Rather, those saying no were the westerners who knew and believed in the importance of indigenous sustainability, and who sat on boards alongside Russians.

We're greatly responsible for either helping or hurting the bride of Christ with our use or misuse of great resources. As I heard the uncle of Spiderman say, "With great power, comes great responsibility." Of course, he was echoing Jesus' words: "From everyone who has been given much, much will be required" (Luke 12:48).

On the Indian Front

Listen to these words of Dr. J. M. Ngul Khan Pau, a native of India, expressing the effect foreign dollars can have in his country:

> Even after 169 years of Christianity, the Assamese Churches (funded by the outside) could not send even a single cross-cultural missionary, whereas the Naga Churches, which completed 130 years, has sent out more than 1,000 missionaries supported by their own local churches. It does not depend on how many years it takes to sponsor a missionary; it has to do with attitude and obedience to the teachings of the Scripture.
>
> The Amri Karbi Christians in Assam will be celebrating their Silver Jubilee next year. Yet till today they cannot even pay the salary of their full-time workers as they are so dependent on the Naga Churches who brought the gospel to them.
>
> The stagnation in growth of the churches in Assam is not because they are poor. It may be because of lack of leadership, but I have seen over the years that it has to do more with financial paternalism.

RAiSE Indigenous Sustainability

There are consultations and workshops we've organized in which we've requested the participants to pay their own travel expenses. It works well, till we have a group coming from overseas paying the Assamese travel expenses and even sitting allowance. While appreciating such good intentions and help, we found out that the next time we asked the delegates to pay their own expenses, they would not come.

Instead of happily participating in fulfilling the Great Commission, they would come out with a long list of reasons why they could not take up such a task. Usually they will ask the same old question, "Who will support or how long will they?" The chronic problem is "dependency" and desire for subsidy from overseas. Such dependent mentality not only stagnated the growth of the church, but alienated those who received "foreign funds" from those who are paid by the local churches.

Some Assamese churches which have wealthy members still do not support even a local pastor, whereas among the tribal churches in Manipur state, even a negligible number of ten families will support a missionary. To my understanding, the main reason is not the wealth and poverty of the church; it has to do with their mentality of dependence. It is not how wealthy the church is but their mental dependence on outside support.

When church leaders' salaries are paid in dollars, which often is several times more than their co-workers, jealousy and strife often ensue. It leads to the professionalization of the clergy. This in turn produces a lot of people who want to go for theological studies because this is the best way to go abroad. Instead of studying and equipping themselves for the ministry, their main aim is to stay as long as possible in the States, from theology to motor-logy, building-ology and dollar-ology.

Leaders who have greased their palms with dollars are not only alienated but they maintain a bureaucratic style of leadership.

What they say is the final word and has to be obeyed. I have heard of severe financial misappropriation in one of the missions in India, where malpractice is known even to the higher leadership and yet corrective measures are not being taken — because he raised more funds than others.

Yet, in the midst of all these, it is very encouraging to know that the Baptist Church of Mizoram celebrated their centenary in 1996. From its inception, the local believers never depended on the contribution of their missionaries except in translation of the Bible and education of the pioneering converts. They started missionary work in the year 1939 and today in 2005 they are working among twenty-five different nationalities and tribes. They have sent out 209 cross-cultural missionaries and 291 working within their own state.

They have missionaries working among Assamese, Arunachalis, Bengalis, Boro, Maharastrian, Madhya Pradesh, Nepalis, Bangladeshi, Chinese, Thai etc. While they have planted 911 new churches in their mission fields, their own local churches are only 405. They have 109,988 new believers in the mission areas; their own membership is just 79,109. The mission budget for this year is Rs. 367,000,000 (US $853,488).

It is no accident that in the Indian sub-continent, we have numerous mission agencies which are directly sustained and funded by generous foreign donors. Such ministries flourish as long as funds are coming. In order to meet the criteria for continuing their funding, some may even go to the extent of buying a congregation by splitting the existing churches. The counting of heads in order to get the continual flow of funds is not the best mission strategy, especially in third world countries. (Taken from the paper "Is Dependency Making Missions Go Sideways?" by Dr. J. M. Ngul Khan Pau of India)

RAiSE Indigenous Sustainability

This is a national worker who has seen the devastating effects of this paternalistic dependency. It reminds me of the proverb, "There is a way which seems right to a man, but its end is the way of death." And again to quote Emerson: "Money often costs too much."

> *Donated money that creates dependency is not merely a waste of money. It's the machete that chops the legs out from under a man.*

Donated money that creates dependency is not merely a waste of money; it's the machete that chops the legs out from under a man. God forbid that we be the ones wielding that machete.

Getting Behind Local Initiative

> When you let money speak for you, it drowns out anything else you meant to say. (Mignon McLaughlin)

> "'Yes,' the king replied, "but to those who use well what they already have, even more will be given." (Jesus)

Money dropped on someone never creates initiative in that person—except perhaps the initiative to go shopping. In fact, it usually does the opposite. People who win the lottery often lose any desire to be productive. Initiative is ruined and lives are more often destroyed than helped.

We see this problem on the reservations set up for Native Americans in the United States. Many of these people have lost the will to work. When we come into an area and start dumping money on a people and on an area, we often can undermine what local initiative is already there.

Money should never be used to create initiative; it should come alongside and empower those who are already taking the initiative. When we partner with someone who's already in motion, our money can serve to empower the already active ministry.

My good friend Shel Arensen is a missionary in Kenya. He has seen money both empower and cripple. When he started reaching out to an unreached people group living in the mountains, he was determined to use his money and resources wisely, and to raise up a church that wouldn't wait for western money before they would act, but would instead take initiative themselves.

Money should never be used to create initiative; it should come alongside and empower those who are already taking the initiative.

As a result, after many had come to faith, he refused to be the one who would build the church building for them—but rather he would help them complete what they'd already begun. Once they put up the walls of the church, Shel said he would come in and put on the tin roof (this also kept them from destroying the vanishing forests around them). Local initiative was encouraged by his actions rather than thwarted.

All too often, we well-intentioned Americans thwart local initiative by simple things like going into a country and constructing a church building. This distinction seems small, but it's profound. One is *coming alongside of,* and the other is *coming in place of.* To fund and help put on the roof is "coming alongside of," but complete funding and building of a church is "coming in place of." One empowers and gives strength; the other takes away and debilitates —even though generous giving is the intention of both.

I sat in the front of a Land-Cruiser as we bumped and banged up the dusty roads from Lake Naivasha into the mountains where the Dorobo lived. These people are extremely self sufficient — one of the few hunter-gatherer people groups left on the planet — but that lifestyle is now rapidly coming to a close as the forest is being torn down around them. As one old Dorobo man put it, "My people had two staples — buffalo meat and honey." Today this diet is supplemented with potatoes they're forced to grow on the deforested land.

I was extremely excited to see a church service among these people who only a decade ago were completely unreached with the gospel. My wife and I joined Shel on a four-hour trek deep into the heart of this people group's territory to visit a new church that had been planted. Shel, who had started the work among the Dorobo, was very anxious to see this church he had never seen. It was one that the Dorobo themselves had planted without the help of any white man. They'd evangelized the area themselves and discipled the folks in the area, and had even built themselves a church building without the help of any white man and without the help of any outsider's money.

We finally arrived and pulled into what would serve as the "church parking lot" in these mountains some 8,000 feet above sea level. It had just enough room for one car. We were the first white faces ever to step into this little church.

The property for the building had been donated by a man who lived nearby and who had just recently come to faith in Christ. The materials had all been gathered locally, and the community came together to build this little building. Not only had they put up the walls, but they hadn't even waited for Shel and his money from abroad to put on the roof.

What a wonderful time of worship we had there.

Such local initiative was amazing to me. I'd just traveled in a neighboring country where the greatest frustration for one of the local native church trainers was the fact that local church initiative had been killed by foreign "Christian welfare." Their attitude was, "Let's wait to see what the foreigners will give."

I asked Shel what he'd done to encourage such local initiative. He replied, "It hasn't been that easy. A few years back I'd just helped complete the roof on a new church. The local leaders asked me then if I could help with an outhouse for the church. I replied, 'You can do that. You build them all the time.' They'd heard about the ways in the rest of Kenya, where the foreigners often give whatever you ask. So they lit into me. 'Pastor Shel, we thought you would help us out more than this.' They were very upset. It wasn't that I couldn't come up with the money or even the laborers. It was the principle of letting them do what they're capable of, and not creating an attitude of needing the 'rich man.'

"I felt horrible, for these men were visibly upset that I was unwilling to help financially with the small task. They went away angry—and they left the church and fell back into their sinful ways of drunkenness and other things. I was devastated. Had I caused these men to fall away? Should I have given them the few dollars they were asking for? Would they have continued walking with the Lord if I had? All these questions nagged at me.

"Well, the local body pitched in, and they built themselves an outhouse, and the church continued on. A couple of years later, these men I'd angered got tired of living in the sin they'd returned to, and they came to the Lord.

"Now, seeing this church that has been completely built with their own hands with no outside assistance, I can rejoice to know that my decision wasn't in vain.

"Another time a group of the Dorobo evangelists asked if I could help out on the next outreach. I said, 'Sure. How can I help?' They asked if I could drive them to the village where they wished to do outreach. The problem with that, I figured, is that if I offered to drive them, they would then think they can do outreach only when they have a car. Obviously I have to drive to even get into the Dorobo country because my home is hours away. But their way of life isn't built around cars; why should the way they do ministry be so?

"I asked them where they wanted to do this outreach, and I volunteered to help. We met in their village, and I walked with them—the fifteen miles or so—and helped share the gospel within this new area.

"Had I driven them that one time, I'm afraid they would have learned the wrong lesson. Now if I occasionally drive them here or there, it doesn't take away their local initiative. They've planted—and always without a car.

When Less Is Truly More

Imagine reading this headline in the morning paper: "Bill Gates Finds Religion; Announces He's Going Back to Church." What would the local churches think if he lived in your city and he made this announcement? What would you hope for?

I would reflect, "Wow, if he's obedient to tithe, that would be some fifty million dollars a year coming into our church. Just think what we could do with all that money! We could finish the building project that's looming over us. And we could just make a killing on our special global outreach offerings." I might cross my fingers and pray he comes our way.

In reality, however, if he did choose my church, and if he did start tithing, I could think of nothing that would be more likely to destroy our church.

Just recently we've had a financial mini-crisis at our church, and we really had to cut our budget. What seemed to be a crisis was truly a great blessing. We'd gotten into the habit of seeing a need and hiring for the position simply because there was always

> *In reality, however, if Gates did choose my church, and if he did start tithing— I could think of nothing that would be more likely to destroy our church.*

enough money there. But now, because financial resources weren't as plentiful as they had been, we were forced to look toward another resource—our people. We needed volunteers, so we went after them. There are more people doing ministry at our church than ever before, and it was because of the lack of funds. People who were in the habit of giving were also giving at a new level of sacrifice than ever before. So just think of our human tendency if Bill Gates were to come here and start tithing.

I recently asked a group of generous and giving Christians: "What would happen if Bill Gates started coming to your church and started tithing his fifty million a year?"

These were their answers:

- People would stop giving to the church.

- People would say to themselves, "What's my $400 a month going to add to the five million already there?"

- People would lose a sense of ownership for the church.

RAiSE Indigenous Sustainability

- People would look for other things to give toward.

- It would ruin the church.

Like I said, unless a church is extremely healthy, this could likely be the beginning of a rapid end.

Should these people stop giving just because Bill shows up on Sunday? Of course not. But the reality is that many would.

Now if these things would happen in a culture where there's already an established tradition of tithing, how much more so if the principle of tithing has never been learned?

It would be a lot like these folks we read about who win the lottery. They hoped they would win so their problems would disappear, and when they do win, the money destroys all that they once had.

When we, as Americans, show up on the scene in a third world country, we're viewed in the same way that we might view Bill Gates: *The rich man is here to save us.* Often the idea exists that we could solve all our problems if the rich guy gets his cash involved. Such a thought is at best a happy delusion.

We do what works for the moment and seems expedient, but it ends up crippling the church—the bride of Christ.

Indigenous sustainability. This was Paul's model. We've had it sitting in front of us for two thousand years. If we ignore it and do our own thing, or if we simply do what seems expedient and works for the moment, we will end up crippling the church—the bride of Christ.

We must ask ourselves the tough questions. Will this project continue if the money dries up tomorrow? Will the locals carry the torch—or is the torch I hand them made from western gold, and too heavy for them to carry? Is what I am doing now undermining the local church's future?

Let's give in a way that builds strong legs to stand on.

A Rotten Foundation

I remember as a kid helping my grandfather, my dad, and my uncle pour a foundation for our 400-square-foot family cabin in the Big Horn Mountains of Wyoming. A thirty-by-thirteen-foot foundation may not seem a big deal, but this one was no easy task. This was because the cabin was already there—fully built—but with no foundation. The bottom logs were sitting right there on the rocky soil.

I remember the fun we had mixing the sand and rocks with the cement, then pouring it into the forms. But my father remembers something different. He remembers the pain it was to get the cabin jacked up, to dig the trenches, set the forms under the jacked-up cabin, then pour the cement, let it set, and then lower the cabin once again. The obvious question the adults were asking was this: Why didn't the guy who built the cabin lay the right foundation to begin with?

Is the money being spent to build big and tall and fast? Or is it being spent to build the right foundation?

The way we spend our money in helping to advance and build the kingdom of God should continually be evaluated. Is the money being spent to build big and tall and fast? Or is it being spent to build the right foundation? My observation is that it's almost always spent to build big, tall, and fast—which of course means that in the long run, lacking a foundation, it can't get big and tall at all.

RAiSE Indigenous Sustainability

Let me explain.

Kazakhstan

Recently, a friend who has been working in the country of Kazakhstan for the past fourteen years was back in the U.S visiting. When he first arrived in Kazakhstan in 1993, there were just a handful of believers in the entire region. In ten short years the number swelled to 15,000. In the last several years, however, the church hasn't grown numerically. In fact, my friend said, the numbers have perhaps even decreased.

This was disappointing to hear, of course. I asked him, "Dave, what do you attribute this to?"

I was rather shocked at how quickly he answered.

"There's no longer a reward of monetary gain if you become a believer. So the church has stopped growing."

> "There's no longer a reward of monetary gain if you become a believer. So the church has stopped growing."

How can this be? What kind of financial gain was there in the first place? Could the way we are giving really stop the growth of the church? These are the questions I threw at him. Here's what Dave described:

With the fall of communism, Kazakhstan opened up to missionaries for the first time in decades. Western missionaries flooded in. The first and only exposure Kazakhstan nationals had to Christians was to people who got paid to be full-time Christians. Immediately, even though it never was spoken, there was an underlying assumption that people get paid to be Christians.

This underlying assumption was reinforced by what happened next in the genesis of the Kazakh church. When the first Kazakhs came to faith in Christ, they were almost immediately rewarded with full-time employment. The missionaries couldn't stand to let such young vibrant believers get lost into the world of work, when they could spend their lives in full-time Christian work. Again it was our western attitude that full-time ministry is superior to part-time. So part of the definition of "Christian" became - something you get paid to be.

Then there was the great pressure to hire your first converts to work for you. Why? Well, if you didn't hire him, the missionary down the street would. These early believers often spoke English, so they knew the foreigners around and had engaged in conversations with them to practice their English. So even though it was Joe who led Ahmet to Christ, and although Joe didn't believe in immediately hiring a new believer, Ahmet had also met with John down the street. John desperately wanted to hire a national to do the full-time work of spreading the gospel. After all, nationals can do it so much cheaper, they already speak the language fluently, and there are plenty of people wanting to get the best bang for the buck back in the U.S who would support Ahmet to become a full-time Christian worker.

Joe was horrified that he would lose his own spiritual child to the guy down the street because Ahmet needed a job and jobs are hard to come by. So either he had to go against his values and hire Ahmet, or let an agency that didn't share his values hire Ahmet. A third option – trying to convince

After all—serving Jesus full-time and getting paid handsomely to do so? Why not?

Ahmet that he didn't need to do this full-time—wasn't so likely. After all—serving Jesus full-time and getting paid handsomely to do so? Why not?

So after having a church system start this way, what would stop it from continuing this way? The western money that had started this machine has now slowly been drying up. The foundation that was laid was laid hastily with the thought that the faster the gospel spread the better. The foundation was built with western money, and when the money dried up, the building stopped.

Many a Kazakh pastor no longer desires to pastor, for his local congregation can't pay him what he became accustomed to living on. And that very congregation that can't pay him has never learned to give of their resources, because the West had underwritten everything in their church.

It's true the building went up fast, but it can only get so tall and so large when it's built on the money from the West. And the problem is this: How easy is it to move a ten-story building from one foundation to another?

Not Just the Third World

The same has been true in other countries. Slovenia opened up to missionaries about the same time as Kazakhstan, but economically was far better off. One might be inclined to think that the church there wouldn't need western financial assistance and that the people could support their own pastors. But it's not whether a country has money—it's what kind of foundation is laid by the missionaries and their money.

A Slovenian Christian told me that the Slovenian pastor of his church told the congregation these very words: "You don't need to give; I can raise the money from the West." Sure enough, he did get the money from America — from three different American churches who supported him personally. Not one of the American churches was aware that there were two other American churches supporting

him as well. And you can guess the health of this church. With no accountability between the pastor and his church, the church was split, factioned, splintered, and broken into pieces.

So back to my original cabin story. Why didn't the guy who built the cabin lay the right kind of foundation in the first place?

My guess is that it was because of the effort and time required to do the digging and haul the cement. What a pain to travel the thirty miles down the mountain to Sheridan to buy cement! The amount needed would require several wagons full, and the horses would have to take it up the steep road. It was so much faster and easier to chop down the logs there and throw the cabin up. There was no thought about longevity.

That's exactly what we're doing when we go in and use our money to hire locals to build the church. We get a lot done fast, but after ten years, we wonder: Why has the church stopped growing? In fact, why is it shrinking? Then we have to go back, jack up the whole cabin, and pour a different foundation.

Let's pour the right foundation right from the beginning.

Paul did this very thing. Let's learn from him.

Look at his life. He was all about foundation. Getting it right the first time. Listen to these words:

For you yourselves know how you ought to follow our example, because we did not act in an undisciplined manner among you, nor did we eat anyone's bread without paying for it, but with labor and hardship we kept working night and day so that we would not be a burden to any of you; not because we do not have the right to this, but in order to offer ourselves as a model for you, so that you would follow our example. (2 Thessalonians 3:7-14)

From the very beginning, Paul modeled work. Paul the "hard core missionary" modeled hard work. Those he led to Christ were not immediately hired to do the job of evangelism. They worked as well, and did the ministry both through their work and on the side. The church members all had to learn to give. There was no Big Brother from the West giving for them. First, they gave to take care of widows and orphans, then to pay those elders who spent a lot of time teaching. Later, perhaps, buildings were built.

Let us wind the clock back before Paul. What's the first example of work in the Scriptures? Genesis 1. *God* worked. God actually had a job. He modeled work and rest. God worked showing us an example to follow. And Paul worked, showing us an example to follow.

We western missionaries can often have this backwards. With money being one of our abundant natural resources, it has traditionally led the charge. We've gone into a country and used western funds to build a church building first. We then find a seemingly trustworthy national and pay him western money to be a full-time pastor. And then, when we see the locals aren't giving to the poor and widows and orphans, we figure it's because they're too poor, and so we go in and use western money to do that for them as well. The locals have never owned the church, and with such a foundation it will never be locally owned. The gospel may have been preached, but it's not being lived. No one has yet shown them how.

The Great Commission says we must teach them to do all that Jesus commanded. Teaching starts with modeling. God knew we needed this, and He started off with work. Paul knew this: "Not because we don't have the right to this, but in order to offer ourselves as a model for you, so that you would follow our example."

"Tent-making" isn't a necessary evil.

Two thousand years later, perhaps we need to learn this again.

"Tent-making" isn't a necessary evil. Paul didn't do it because he needed the money, but, as he said, "in order to be a model for you. So you would follow our example."

If the early missionaries in a culture are all full-time, paid evangelists, then that will be the model they've learned. It's the law of first impressions. This model is dependent on foreign funds. If, however, the first Christians they meet are teaching and working hard for the good of the society and sharing their faith with everyone and leading Bible studies in their home, then a model has been set up from the beginning that's not dependent on foreign money. The locals can all do this. And they will.

In a culture where there was no full-time Christian ministry, Paul came in just like them—a worker. He reached them while being one of them.

In a culture where there was no full-time Christian ministry, Paul came in just like them—a worker. He reached them while being one of them. They could immediately do what he did without foreign funds. As the church grew, soon natural leaders and teachers would emerge. Then Paul said there were elders who preach and teach who were worthy of double honor. The local church could decide: "Let's pay this guy to do it full-time." It wasn't an outside choice. It was an indigenous one. He wasn't paid from outside, but by his own. He was accountable to his own. It had become truly indigenous, in a culture that would make much of our third world look modern.

So when it comes to laying a foundation, we must do what the man who built our family cabin did not. We must use our money to go back down the mountain to buy the right kind of cement. It may be hard to get it up the face of the mountain, and the horses might die trying, but this cement is critical. The right kind of sand and the right kind of rock must be thrown into the mixer. A solid and lasting foundation must be poured.

It still takes money to build the cabin, but the money must be spent for the right things at the right time. Even if the cabin doesn't get built this year, it's better to have one that will survive the hard winters and the test of time. We need a foundation that will not rot in a few short years.

A Timely Example

As soon as I finished writing the content above, the following message came in by e-mail from one of our church's missionaries. It shows what happens when the structure of a national ministry is laid on the foundation of foreign money. This is a very good national leader and one of the most reputable mission agencies we've worked with. I do think, however, the agency laid a shaky foundation built on foreign bank notes rather than on indigenous cement. Real names are changed.

Hey there. Really hope you're doing well. We're doing well, but wanted to share about some things to pray about. There's definite tension with us and Petras in regard to finances.

Our general philosophies are polar opposites. His and the other national workers' hearts — for the most part — are TOTALLY in the right place, but when it comes to spending money (personal or ministry), he/they spend freely relying on the hope that foreign money will come in. My agency is trying not to feed this habit...in fact, they've insisted that it stop and that many financial practices (such as tracking) improve. But I (Samuel) am getting the brunt of the frustration from Petras because these changes came at about the same time we arrived (and I'm in charge of finances for everyone here). It seems so basic to me that you can only spend what you have even if that means you need to say "no" to some people who want to attend this or that, but don't have the money. Petras simply does not want to say "no" to anyone, and will "rob Peter to pay Paul" ...but this can't happen any more.

Anyway, some of this came up recently as we near a big Youth Leader Conference where western money has always paid for folks to come, and we had a BIG discussion today where I shared with him frustrations about how these things are not right. This area we want to ask you to pray for. Really, your prayers mean a lot...

We love and appreciate all of you!
In His Prayerful Service,
Samuel

My reply:

Hey Samuel,
Remember this fact: as long as foreign money pays the bulk for an indigenous conference — it really is very much a foreign conference.

The best way to become truly indigenous is to start out that way. Get the locals to figure out a way to pay for things or figure out ways to do things that don't cost so much.

Believe it or not, if it starts dependent on western money — western money will eventually end it.

Petras' attitude is like that of a little kid who has had his bedtime candy taken away from him. First of all, he should never have been given candy at bedtime. Second of all, for health's sake it should be taken away immediately. And third, any kid who was raised on candy at bedtime is going to scream if you take it away. Explaining to him why it's for his own good is important, but not easily understood.

So don't get mad at Petras. He has been weaned on western candy and it is the giver of that candy who is to blame. So it is a good thing to wean them from the candy, but even better to never let them taste it. He is experiencing what is completely natural but very hard. Chances are his own salary comes from the West as well, and you can bet he will scream when the time comes for that to be taken away.

In my opinion, it is best to not start things this way. It is best to start them in a way that is compatible with the local economy and the local level of giving. This is how Paul did it.

I am sorry if this is an oversimplification of the problem—but I have seen it happen what seems a hundred times in the last couple of years. And yes, we will pray.

Jonathan

Weaning Nationals Off the Foreign Bottle

My father just returned from India training pastors in a school there. The school has approached supporting the newly graduated pastors in two different ways. One was a five-year plan: Total foreign-raised support the first year, down to 80 percent foreign the second year and 60 percent the third, until by the end of the fifth year they're required to be fully supported indigenously. The idea is that the church would then be in a position to support them.

The other plan was the bi-vocational model. Here, they'll work a job to support themselves while they are alos pastoring.

I asked my father which works better. Without hesitation, he said the bi-vocational pastor was more successful and the churches did better. This pastor is also more likely to be fully supported after five years by the church he starts. His church has accepted him from the beginning—"He's one of us"—and they've taken ownership of him. So it's a good thing to wean them from the bottle, but even better to never let them taste the milk.

> *So it's a good thing to wean them from the bottle, but even better to never let them taste the milk.*

RAISE Indigenous Sustainability

Chapter Ten

RAIS*E*: Equity
Bringing People Together — Not Pushing Them Apart

Equity: 1): the quality of being fair or impartial;
fairness; impartiality: the equity of Solomon;
2): something that is fair and just.

ONLINE DICTIONARY

The King is mighty, he loves justice—you have
established equity; in Jacob you have done
what is just and right.

ANCIENT HEBREW PSALM

We rightfully get offended when we see "Christians" on TV with their $3,000 suits, a diamond-studded watch, and huge gems on every finger, sitting on furniture no mere mortal can afford. We cry out in disdain, "This is a health-and-wealth gospel!"

Yet we are often guilty of sending nationals back to their country with cars, clothes, and enough wealth (personal financial support) to buy a rich man's house. Not by our standards of course; but in that country, the only standards that count are the local ones. We have, by our giving, elevated the minister to an economic class sometimes high above those he ministers to. We give cars to ministers who live in cultures that cannot afford a bike. We give $500 a month to men who minister to a culture where the average pastor makes less than a dollar a day.

This encourages people in that country to go into ministry for the financial reward they've seen their leaders gain. Unfortunately, many in third world do just that.

The thought is this: "Let's become pastors with connections to America and we can be rich." We generously and unknowingly have fed and continue to feed a health-and-wealth gospel in the third world.

> We generously and unknowingly have fed and continue to feed a health-and-wealth gospel in the third world.

This is why it's important for _relationship_ to precede giving. Without relationship, it's impossible to know the effects of our giving—whether they're helpful or harmful.

A missionary from our church told me about a well-meaning westerner who felt compassion on a poor church in the third world. There were some evangelists in the church that had a heart for God. This man thought of how much more effective they would be if they had bicycles. And he bought two bicycles for the two evangelists. He had no idea that what he'd done would cause a huge fight within the church. In this culture, the old are to be honored first, and the gifts should never go to younger men. The younger men also were able to use the bicycles for their farming work, transporting seed and vegetables to market, giving them great advantage over others in the church. The older ones felt hurt and angered about the lack of respect this generous man had shown, and there was great inequity created.

This isn't to say that giving the bicycles was bad—but it could have been done in a way that didn't create the inequities. This again shows the great need for a cultural expert to be involved to keep us from creating needless rifts in Christ's body, the church. And these were just bicycles. Westerners are often buying cars for these guys. Imagine the inequities.

> At this present time your abundance being a supply for their need, so that their abundance also may become a supply for your need, that there may be equality; as it is written, "He who gathered much did not have too much, and he who gathered little had no lack. (2 Corinthians 8:14-15)

Churches Helping Churches: "Nothing but Good Intentions"

A well-meaning generous church from the United States headed to Mexico to help our brothers in the South. They did what many churches do—built a building for a small body of believers. After all, a church needs a building, right?

These Americans worked hard. Poured sweat and even some blood into this place. After some time of hard work, the building was done. They were overjoyed—the Americans that is. The Mexican brothers and sisters smiled and shook hands and politely thanked them for coming and helping them. They bid their farewells, hugged, said "good-bye, adios," and then said them all again. And again.

The Americans hopped in their van and headed back to the United States where no doubt they showed their slide shows and encouraged others to step out for the Lord. Their lives truly would never be the same again.

Little did these Americans know that as soon as they left, the smiles on the faces of their Mexican "sister church" disappeared as they walked over to their new building and began to take it apart piece by piece. Reusing the materials, they rebuilt the building the way they wanted it, in the place they wanted it.

No one can doubt the generosity and the good intentions of the American church group. They'd given thousands of dollars and hours of hardship and toil. Did it accomplish anything good? Absolutely —it changed the hearts of the Americans. They broke out of their selfish world and learned to give. That's a major accomplishment. But did it really help the locals? Yes, in a way. It gave them some raw materials to work with. I guess that can count as good.

The above story is true. It's not really that rare to have this happen—things like this occur often when a western church goes into a third world country without any cultural expertise. The money given to such projects always has a profound impact on the ones giving, but it often damages —for the long term—the ones receiving such well intended, but ultimately "thoughtless", aid.

> Cultural expertise is needed. Someone is needed to act as the bridge to help connect the two cultures.

Cultural expertise is needed. Someone is needed to act as the bridge to help connect the two cultures. Language is only part of this. In fact, it's not even the major part.

The word *expert* in English is related to the word "experience." Someone who has studied the local language in a school back in the States is not an expert. Someone who has been on five short-term teams to a given area is not an expert. But someone who has lived and worked with a given people group for a great many years —this is the true meaning of a cultural expert. This is the kind of person who's needed to help a western church give in a way that's constructive, rather than destructive.

That's why our churches need to have long-term missionaries on the ground. They become the experts, and we can send our summer teams through them—with them acting as the bridge for us to get across the cultural chasms.

Many people believe that if they can just find a good English speaker in the host country, that person can act as the expert. This is just not so. They don't understand Americans. They quickly come to understand that Americans will dump money on them just because they like you, and these "bridges" are often corrupted and destroyed by generous Americans.

Want to Start a Fight?

I remember traveling through Burundi, which according to the World Almanac is the poorest country on the planet, in GNP per capita income. I saw many children who were hungry. At a border crossing we were forced to stop for about an hour, and a small group of the cutest kids gathered around our car. My eye caught the two littlest in the bunch. Their little stomachs were bloated due to malnourishment. And there on my lap before me were some Digestive Biscuits (the British equivalent to our graham cracker).

I'd asked Tambry, who was my cultural expert friend, if it was okay to give them some crackers. She said it wouldn't be smart.

That just sounded so selfish to me. Here were hungry kids, and I had some crackers. Yet someone tells me, "Don't give them away."

I hoped Tambry would look away so I could hand these kids the crackers. In my mind, this "expert" friend had grown a little too callous to the needs of these people.

Well, I decided to do it my way, and I reached out and gave these cute little runny-nosed boys the crackers and...

Kaboom—the fight was on. Some big kids saw us hand out the goods and ran over, knocking a little kid down, fighting over the fallen crackers while another little guy ran off trying desperately to stuff his face before he fell victim to the same cruel fate.

It was truly one of the saddest things I've ever seen. I meant it for good, but my good intentions had started a fight.

Tambry, my cultural expert, knew this would happen, and that's why she said it wouldn't be smart. It had nothing to do with a calloused heart—she simply could foresee

> It was truly one of the saddest things I've ever seen. I meant it for good, but my good intentions had started a fight.

exactly what would happen. She knew that a few graham crackers would do nothing to help the child and his malnourishment, and she knew it would cause a fight. The cultural ignoramus that I was said, "I want to love these kids with an act of kindness."

My generosity will be rewarded. My wisdom—not.

The irony of this story is that Tambry and Dan (her husband) are doing more to eliminate hunger and childhood disease by empowering the local church than probably anyone in the country. They've given up their prosperous American lives to be there to help. They obviously care about these people, for I'd seen it time and again, and I should have trusted that she knew what she was talking about when I asked about giving away the crackers.

Now, I'd already lived overseas for eleven years when I made that mistake. How much more prone to mistakes are churches who don't know a wink about cross-cultural work. We are destined to make a mess—unless we are teachable and look to the counsel of a cultural expert.

The expert is needed. Why not let it be one of your own? Send out people from your church. Get them on the ground for long-term work with an organization that has a good reputation of planting and working with the indigenous church. Then send your short-term teams to empower the work God is already doing through your own people and the churches they work with.

Who is an expert?

Missionary kids who grew up playing with the locals, then spent time back here in the U.S., then ended up back on the field as adults have always impressed me as the greatest experts. They know the language, and they know the hearts of the people on both sides of the ocean. Not all missionary kids have spent time among the locals, and some don't even speak the local languages, but those who do are among the best experts I've met. They tend to love the people around them because they've grown up with them.

Long term missionaries, relief workers, and teachers—those who have served overseas for a long time and know the local languages well. The more they've seen of other various cultures just adds to their expertise. Always make sure they exhibit a love and compassion for those around them.

Workers, both native and foreign, from reputable agencies who have been well taught and trained in culture. Someone who has been under the direction and teaching of someone who really knows their stuff can serve well as an expert.

Who is *not* an expert?

Someone who has read about the place and people online is not. Nor is someone who has been on several short-term teams to a given area, or someone who only learned the language in school. Though these people have learned much and may have much to share, they often assume the role of an expert because they know facts—but facts cannot substitute for knowledge and expertise which comes only from experience

There's no substitute for expertise. If you partner with a church of another culture without the appropriate experts helping you understand, you'll do harm with your generous giving. You can be sure of that much.

Now back to an earlier story that may have left you scratching your head. How could a church be destroyed by a team from America generously giving of their time and resources by building a simple church building and a small dwelling for the Mexican pastor and his family?

> *If you partner with a church of another culture without the appropriate experts helping you understand, you'll do harm with your generous giving. You can be sure of that much.*

First, it raised the pastor to a level higher than those he ministered to, creating an artificial inequity.

Second, the building wasn't a product of the locals' own vision, giving, and hard work. In other words, it had nothing to do with them at all, but everything to do with America. It left the locals wondering, "Whose church is this anyway?"

Third, the pastor was then seen as an American puppet. He'd kissed up to the wealthy class. He was seen as doing what he did to get ahead, and all indications were that somehow he'd sold out to American ways, customs, and cash. He was no longer of the people —but of a foreign people. The church was no longer a local one. It was strange and foreign in every respect.

This thriving third world church was torn apart—all on the foundation of generous and good intentions. These generous men who made this mistake, have learned from this and continue to give in ways that really help. May we all learn from them.

A Note to Short Term Teams

We have had teams working with the Karamajong tribe in Uganda - a notorious violent people that until recently have been killing themselves off at an alarming rate. Our first teams into the area were warned by our local expert to not give any money away – which is our first tendency when we see the extreme poverty. So instead, suitcases of extra clothing were given as the team left, wrist watches taken off and given to the tribe chiefs and pastors, and other items that seemed frivolous and harmless to these team members after seeing the poverty and hardship that the locals daily endured. Our expert was later able to describe to us the negative impact of these seemingly harmless gifts. They created petty jealousies and helped work against the very peace our teams came to preach.

These team leaders now have a policy for all teams going into the region – take only love and the Gospel. Let the expert – Val Shean - a Veterinarian who has lived among these people for 14 years – distribute any money or gifts you want to give. It has taken her this many years to know how to do it right. The team gave Val several Leatherman tools to give to the warriors who came to the peace talks. It is now eight months later and she still has them. It was neither the time nor place to give them during the peace talks. Only Val – who has lived with them – could know that.

Just eight months after these peace talks (where the gifts were not handed out) there are 7000 Karmajong from previously warring clans now living in peace in thirty-nine village. The Ugandan government is shocked and the U.N. dumbfounded. Val has been a model of helping me understand how the RAISE principles work.

She refuses to create inequities.

Our teams must resist the urge to give gifts and cash to the needy, and instead must trust the expert - our veterinarian friend - to be the expert.

So short term teams beware. Your small and large gifts may be going to undermine the very thing you came to do. Don't make a short term error that may have long term negative consequences. If there is no cultural expert to help you know if what you are giving away is wise – then be wise and don't give where you don't have understanding.

RAIse Equity

Part III:

—

Building on
the Big Four

Chapter Eleven

Child Sponsorships

Debilitating Welfare or Life-Empowering Change?

If I have raised my hand against the
fatherless, knowing that I could have defended
them, then let my arm fall from the shoulder,
let it be torn off at the joint.

THE BOOK OF JOB

Whoever causes one of these little ones who
believe in Me to stumble, it is better for him
that a heavy millstone be hung around his
neck, and that he be drowned in the depth of
the sea.

JESUS

Childhood sponsorship programs are wildly popular and
generate income for relief agencies unlike any other program.
As a result, many relief and development agencies are jumping on
the bandwagon and starting their own sponsorship programs. Other
compassionate people with no relief and development expertise are
starting up their own programs from scratch.

Some of these experienced programs are excellent. But many—
in their effort to do good—are tearing at the very fabric of society
by exporting a welfare system that closely resembles that which has

miserably failed in the United States. In order for there to be long-term sustainable benefit for a society, these programs have got to keep the four points of RAISE before them. Some do. Many do not. All of these agencies can and should be about the business of improvement.

RAISE: Relationship

Perhaps the greatest strength of child sponsorship programs is the *relationship* that's brought about. We in the materialistic West are suddenly connected by a relationship with someone from a truly needy part of the world. This relationship costs money, and there's nothing wrong with that. It's only through relationship that the love of Christ becomes incarnate, which doesn't happen when money is simply thrown at a problem.

Childhood sponsorships connect cultures in a way that very rarely happens in any other form of giving. Consider the vast difference in the two following prayers — one general, one relational:

1) Dear Lord, I know there are hungry people out there. So take my gift — this check I am writing — and use it somewhere on someone who needs it. I trust your will. Amen.

2) Dear Lord, I pray for Marium. Thank you that she is now able to go to school and for the role I got to play in this. Thank you that she is no longer hungry at night and for the fact that she has not had to be hospitalized in these two years that I have been able to be involved in her life. Thank you God for this beautiful picture on my fridge that she drew herself and for the sweet thank you notes. God, thank you for letting me be involved in her life. Thanks for the opportunity I have to write this check and this letter

this month. Amen.

And on Marium's side, it's the same. She sees the money not coming from some organization, but from an individual who's writing, praying, and giving to her needs in the name of Christ.

It's true, a large percentage of the thirty dollars per month goes to maintain the relationship. But relationship is worth paying for.

RAISE: Accountability

Most well known organizations involved with childhood sponsorships give money in an accountable fashion. A good organization should be up front about the cost breakdown, telling you how much of your thirty dollars per month goes to food, education, community development, healthcare, and keeping you informed.

You should ask about these things. You're a steward over your money. If an organization is unwilling or unable to answer your question, you shouldn't be giving to them. It might mean they're embarrassed or ashamed about the way it's used, or it might simply mean that they're not organized enough to know how the money is spent. Either way, it is probably not a wise investment. See if you agree with the ways your money is allocated.

RAISE: Indigenous Sustainability

I've found that many childhood sponsorship programs do not do a good job in this area. Remember that unless the goal is to create financial sustainability and to empower this child to be taken care of in the context of her local community, then we're creating a system of dependency.

We must remember that there's no guarantee that the organization through whom you choose to give will be able to continue giving in this context indefinitely. They may be asked to leave the country tomorrow, and if that's the case—and the money you've given has brought no sustainable change—then the child is no better off than she was before you began giving.

I was just talking to a man about this very thing. The political winds changed, and a child sponsorship program had to be abruptly ended. The families had learned to totally depend on this outside help, and as a result, were less prepared to deal with life (growing their own food and making their own money) than those who hadn't received the help. Is this the best stewardship of money— that those who had received it became less equipped to deal with life than those who did not?

On the other hand, there are sponsorships which go to develop and train those who are destitute in the basics of how to care for themselves, and these sponsorships provide infrastructure that can help fully support the weight of the society even after the source of outside money dries up. The only problem with this empowering and lasting kind of development is that it takes considerably more work and thought on behalf of the agency that runs the sponsorship. It's much easier just to come in and feed and pay for school than to actually get the local community to pull together so they can bear their own weight.

> *It's much easier just to come in and feed and pay for school than to actually get the local community to pull together so they can bear their own weight.*

The cost of not doing this correctly can be great. To simply come in and do everything for them by financially underwriting it all will pretty much guarantee that they never learn to do these things on their own. After all, why should I learn to pay and work for my food and education when someone else is doing it for me free of charge?

If we really don't want to feed such debilitating attitudes creating sick systems of dependency with our generosity, we must ask these agencies the hard questions:

- How does this program seek to get the children out of a cycle of dependency?

- How does it encourage work?

- How does it keep the responsibility upon the shoulders of the parents and the society to take care of its own?

- What time frame does the agency have for getting the community to stand on its own feet so sponsorship is no longer needed in a given village?

If an agency cannot answer these questions, then chances are they're creating more long-term problems and a culture of dependency. Your money will simply be creating a bigger black hole that will require even more money.

In the United States, the welfare system provided funds for mothers without jobs and without husbands. This seemed good on the surface; after all, they're in need. But what this practice does is send this message: We, the government, will pay you if you have children with no husband, but we won't pay you if you do have a husband. We'll pay you to not work, but we won't pay you if you do work.

Women actually get paid to leave their husbands. Others actually get paid to leave their jobs.

GIVING WISELY?

This policy sends a message that has the power to destroy. Women actually get paid to leave their husbands. Others actually get paid to leave their jobs. This was the message that was heard.

As a result many women have sent their husbands away and divorced them so they could get "paid." Because the government would now fill that role, the husband was no longer needed to provide. Women were no longer encouraged to work, because as soon as they began, they lost their "free" handout.

The sociological damage that has been done in the United States as a result of empowering the "absent father" and empowering a listless work ethic has been far greater than perhaps we will ever know. It has torn at the very fabric of our society leaving a social mess in its wake.

I've heard Christians rail against the welfare system here in the United States and about how it has created a system of rewarding bad and sociologically damaging behavior. I've yet to meet a Christian who has even hinted that this has been a good thing. Even those who were once proponents of the welfare system have now tried to reform it. But—tragically—many childhood sponsorships are following this same disproven pattern.

Consider the following scenario for a sponsorship program that targets widows and orphans. The message going out is this: If you're a widow, your child can be sponsored; if you have a husband, your child cannot. Those who have a husband see the widow's children growing healthy and fat on foreign dollars, and the husband sees the same. Can you blame the husband for leaving, or the wife for sending him away?

You may think this doesn't happen, but it does, and at many

levels. If a "free meal ticket" comes and continues in any form at all, it will bring a heavy cost to the local culture. It will tear its very fabric—that very thing which has held it together through even the toughest times.

> *If a 'free meal ticket' comes and continues in any form at all, it will bring a heavy cost to the local culture.*

I recently sat across from Samuel, a Zimbabwe citizen, at a relief conference. These were his words. "I have seen Sponsorships come in and tell a father he is no longer needed." He was angry.

As Christians we must give in ways that keep the good cultural fabric intact, and we must give in ways that lift the whole village up together so it can stand on its own feet together. We also must weave those Christian elements into the fabric so the village can stand firm together. Many sponsorship programs are doing this very poorly and are creating long-term damage. Even the best programs can learn to do this better, and it's your job as a giver to be informed and to encourage improvement

RAISE: Equity

Perhaps an even greater problem than achieving indigenous sustainability is the inequities that can be created if time, thought, and diligent efforts aren't taken to keep such inequities from ripping at the very fabric of a society.

Just last week a young man from a Bible college was promoting his new agency and the work they're doing through child sponsorship. He showed some slides and said, "You can see the difference between the kids in the village—those who are sponsored are healthy, and those who are not are thin and sickly."

Taken one way, these words can mean, "Look at the good we're doing." But taken another way, equally valid, they mean: "Look at the inequities we're creating in this village."

We've got to address this question: What damage is being done to the very fabric of these communal villages by such sponsorship that chooses one child and doesn't choose the child next door? What will be the long-term effects?

As has happened under our own noses here in the U.S., the damage can actually outweigh the good in the long run. If this question hasn't been answered and there seems to be no attempt to answer it—if all you get is a "we'll have to wait and see" answer —then this is probably not an organization with which you should sponsor a child.

A Better Kind of Sponsorship

Avoiding inequities isn't an easy task, but there's no question that it's best to work with the community as a whole rather than singling out individuals for sponsorship.

Unfortunately, sponsoring a village isn't as personal as sponsoring a child. It does not feel the same. I was just at a meeting last week with a relief organization that partners with our church as we reach out to some very needy places in Africa. Historically, this agency hasn't done child sponsorships because of the inequities they almost always have created and the social problems that ensue, but this organization also realizes the ability such a program has in making relationships happen between cultures.

We were brainstorming about possible solutions. One is to financially sponsor an entire village and the projects, which include health and education improvements, but then you sponsor a family in this village with your prayers and encouragement. While the whole village learns to work together to take care of and provide for each other, they're all in touch by writing letters and sending pictures with a family that is praying for them individually. This solution works toward indigenous sustainability and makes equity a priority.

> *If we as Christians continue to export the same irresponsible practice into other cultures, will we not be held accountable?*

All sponsorship programs must act responsibly and not go in and tear apart a culture by exporting the same welfare system we know doesn't work here in the United States. We must do it right. We have a duty before God to help communities and families stay together and to help them grow closer to one another. If we as Christians continue to export the same irresponsible practice into other cultures, will we not be held accountable?

In order to invest wisely we must give to those sponsorship programs that hit on all four cylinders. Ask the questions. Direct your money toward agencies that work responsibly. Don't settle for less. After all, you're investing His money.

Chapter Twelve

Support of Organizations

Well then, you should have put my money on
deposit in the bank, so that when I returned I
would have received it back with interest.

JESUS

The part of the day I seem to dread the most is when I go down
to my mailbox in the copy room here at the church. Why?
Because I know I'll be stuck in that room for the next five, ten, or
even twenty minutes, just sifting through my mail.

Since coming on as the pastor of global outreach at a fairly large
church, I've begun to feel a bit like the wealthy philanthropist must
feel. Everyone wants money.

Some can tell of their need with stories that make you cry.
Others are able to use the power of shear reason to convince you
that it's indeed they who should be the recipients of a large check.
I used to bring the mail up to my office and try to wade through it
there, but then the phone would ring and it would be someone else
—often someone I didn't know asking for money. Then I would have
to leave the office and soon I had a huge mound of mail cluttering
up my desk too overwhelming to even think of going through. So
now this sifting through the requests for checks is all done in the
copy room.

So many of the requests come from Christian organizations.
Many are excellent organizations, and others not so excellent. Some
might rightfully be called scams—and for some that label would be

generous. Even the best are less than perfect.

All these organizations have one thing in common: They need money to function. There's nothing wrong with that. But great difficulty comes when deciding which of these organizations to give to.

A close friend of mine has done extremely well in business, and he's committed to giving a million dollars away over the course of his lifetime. Deciding who to give it to isn't a difficulty for him. He came to faith in Christ through the ministry of a certain organization while in college. He has gotten to know the leadership and has partnered with them in ministry in different parts of the world. He sees all the time how money for this organization goes to work for the kingdom. At the same time, his relationship with leaders allows him to ask the tough questions about why money is being spent on this or that. As a result, his life is being changed in more ways than just writing a check a few times a year.

> *All these organizations have one thing in common: They need money to function.*

I got together with him a few years back, and the stories he told of how God has used him through this ministry because of his business have been incredible. He truly has partnered with this organization, and his giving is an extension of this partnership. This is healthy giving.

Here are important things to think about when deciding whether to give to an organization.

Relationship: Do I have a relationship with them? Do I personally know and trust the leadership of this organization? Does any of my church staff have a relationship with them? Does our church have missionaries with this organization? How can we partner in more than just financial ways?

Accountability: Who's on the board of directors? Are they known men and women of integrity? Are they a member of the Evangelical Council for Financial Accountability (ECFA)? Can they account for funds given to them and show how they've been used?

Indigenous sustainability: Do they have indigenous leadership, or are they run by foreigners? Is this indigenous leadership funded primarily or exclusively with foreign funds? What's the policy for trying to get the locals to raise support from the locals? Is this actually happening?

Equity: How well does this organization allow indigenous workers to continue on at the level of those they minister to? Are people enticed in the third world country to come on staff with this organization for the financial gain and western connections they might have?

How is Jesus honored through this ministry and work?

Chapter Thirteen

Relief and Development Work

> Woe to those who make unjust laws, to those
> who issue oppressive decrees, to deprive the
> poor of their rightsand withhold justice from
> the oppressed of my people, making widows
> their preyand robbing the fatherless.What will
> you do on the day of reckoning, when disaster
> comes from afar? To whom will you run for
> help? Where will you leave your riches?
>
> THE PROPHET ISAIAH

How should we respond to the seemingly multiplying disasters around the world — earthquakes, tsunamis, hurricanes, droughts, famine, war?

One thing is for certain: We need to respond. Jesus says, "Whoever in the name of a disciple gives to one of these little ones even a cup of cold water to drink, truly I say to you, he shall not lose his reward" (Matthew 10:42).

The Bible rings with this truth:

> Inasmuch as you have done it to the least of these, so you have done it to me. (Matthew 25:40)

> He executes justice for the orphan and the widow, and shows His love for the refugee by giving him food and clothing. (Deuteronomy 10:18)

A father of the fatherless and a judge for the widows, is God in His holy habitation. God makes a home for the lonely; He leads out the prisoners into prosperity. (Psalm 68:5-6)

The concept of doing relief and development work "in His name" isn't a small point. In the aftermath of the 2004 tsunami in Southern Asia, many organizations were criticized for bringing a Christian message along with their sacks of grain and helping hands. From the media came the cry, "Just help the people, for goodness sake, and quit trying to proselytize." Such cries come from a materialistic and relativistic worldview. What kind of Christian would I be to feed someone their whole life long and yet never present the gospel to him? Keep them alive so they simply could experience an eternal death away from the presence of their Creator?

In the aftermath of the 2004 tsunami in Southern Asia, many organizations were criticized for bringing a Christian message along with their sacks of grain and helping hands.

If the reason we're there is because of Jesus, we'd better be honest and say so. Otherwise we're taking the glory of this good deed for ourselves and not letting it bring glory to His name.

If an organization is ashamed to proclaim the name of Christ, then I personally am ashamed to give to that organization. If I exist to bring glory to His name, then I should give to an organization that does so.

If the reason we're there is because of Jesus, we'd better be honest and say so. Otherwise we're taking the glory of this good deed for ourselves and not letting it bring glory to His name.

In fact, there's a huge cost when we don't give in His name and seek to give instead through something other than the church for reasons other than the glory of His name.

A friend of mine mailed me an article from the German magazine *Der Spiegel*. The man being interviewed is African, born and raised in Kenya, and he's shouting loudly that government aid must stop. Listen to his reasons why, and ask how the church can be different.

Der Spiegel Interview with African Economics Expert

"For God's Sake, Please Stop the Aid!"

The Kenyan economics expert James Shikwati says that aid to Africa does more harm than good. The avid proponent of globalization spoke with *Der Spiegel* about the disastrous effects of western development policy in Africa, corrupt rulers, and the tendency to overstate the AIDS problem.

SPIEGEL: Mr. Shikwati, the G8 summit at Gleneagles is about to beef up the development aid for Africa...

Shikwati:...for God's sake, please just stop.

SPIEGEL: Stop? The industrialized nations of the West want to eliminate hunger and poverty.

Shikwati: Such intentions have been damaging our continent for the past forty years. If the industrial nations really want to help the Africans, they should finally terminate this awful aid. The countries that have collected the most development aid are also the ones that are in the worst shape. Despite the billions that have poured into Africa, the continent remains poor.

SPIEGEL: Do you have an explanation for this paradox?

Shikwati: Huge bureaucracies are financed (with the aid money), corruption and complacency are promoted, Africans are taught to be beggars and not to be independent. In addition, development aid weakens the local markets everywhere and dampens

> *Despite the billions that have poured into Africa, the continent remains poor.*

the spirit of entrepreneurship that we so desperately need. As absurd as it may sound, development aid is one of the reasons for Africa's problems. If the West were to cancel these payments, normal Africans wouldn't even notice. Only the functionaries would be hard hit. Which is why they maintain that the world would stop turning without this development aid.

SPIEGEL: Even in a country like Kenya, people are starving to death each year. Someone has got to help them.

Shikwati: But it has to be the Kenyans themselves who help these people. When there's a drought in a region of Kenya, our corrupt politicians reflexively cry out for more help. This call then reaches the United Nations World Food Program—which is a massive

> *As absurd as it may sound, development aid is one of the reasons for Africa's problems.*

agency of apparatchiks who are in the absurd situation of, on the one hand, being dedicated to the fight against hunger while, on the other hand, being faced with unemployment were hunger actually eliminated. It's only natural that they willingly accept the plea for more help. And it's not uncommon that they demand a little more money than the respective African government originally requested. They then forward that request to their headquarters, and before long, several thousands tons of corn are shipped to Africa...

SPIEGEL:...corn that predominantly comes from highly-subsidized European and American farmers...

Shikwati:...and at some point, this corn ends up in the harbor of Mombasa. A portion of the corn often goes directly into the hands of unscrupulous politicians who then pass it on to their own tribe to boost their next election campaign. Another portion of the shipment ends up on the black market where the corn is dumped at extremely low prices. Local farmers may as well put down their hoes right away; no one can compete with the UN's World Food Program. And because the farmers go under in the face of this pressure, Kenya would have no reserves to draw on if there actually were a famine next year. It's a simple but fatal cycle.

SPIEGEL: If the World Food Program didn't do anything, the people would starve.

Shikwati: I don't think so. In such a case, the Kenyans, for a change, would be forced to initiate trade relations with Uganda or Tanzania, and buy their food there. This type of trade is vital for Africa. It would force us to improve our own infrastructure, while making national borders—drawn by the Europeans by the way— more permeable. It would also force us to establish laws favoring market economy.

SPIEGEL: Would Africa actually be able to solve these problems on its own?

Shikwati: Of course. Hunger shouldn't be a problem in most of the countries south of the Sahara. In addition, there are vast natural resources—oil, gold, diamonds. Africa is always only portrayed as a continent of suffering, but most figures are vastly exaggerated. In the industrial nations, there's a sense that Africa would go under without development aid. But believe me, Africa existed before you

Europeans came along. And we didn't do all that poorly either.

SPIEGEL: But AIDS didn't exist at that time.

Shikwati: If one were to believe all the horrifying reports, then all Kenyans should actually be dead by now. But now, tests are being carried out everywhere, and it turns out that the figures were vastly exaggerated. It's not three million Kenyans that are infected. All of the sudden, it's only about one million. Malaria is just as much of a problem, but people rarely talk about that.

SPIEGEL: And why's that?

Shikwati: AIDS is big business, maybe Africa's biggest business. There's nothing else that can generate as much aid money as shocking figures on AIDS. AIDS is a political disease here, and we should be very skeptical.

SPIEGEL: The Americans and Europeans have frozen funds previously pledged to Kenya. The country is too corrupt, they say.

> *Unfortunately, the Europeans' devastating urge to do good can no longer be countered with reason.*

Shikwati: I am afraid, though, that the money will still be transferred before long. After all, it has to go somewhere. Unfortunately, the Europeans' devastating urge to do good can no longer be countered with reason. It makes no sense whatsoever that directly after the new Kenyan government was elected—a leadership change that ended the dictatorship of Daniel arap Mois—the faucets were suddenly opened and streams of money poured into the country.

SPIEGEL: Such aid is usually earmarked for a specific objective, though.

Shikwati: That doesn't change anything. Millions of dollars earmarked for the fight against AIDS are still stashed away in Kenyan bank accounts and have not been spent. Our politicians were overwhelmed with money, and they try to siphon off as much as possible. The late tyrant of the Central African Republic, Jean Bedel Bokassa, cynically summed it up by saying, "The French government pays for everything in our country. We ask the French for money. We get it, and then we waste it."

SPIEGEL: In the West, there are many compassionate citizens wanting to help Africa. Each year, they donate money and pack their old clothes into collection bags...

Shikwati:...and they flood our markets with that stuff. We can buy these donated clothes cheaply at our so-called Mitumba markets. There are Germans who spend a few dollars to get used Bayern Munich or Werder Bremen jerseys, in other words, clothes that some German kids sent to Africa for a good cause. After buying these jerseys, they auction them off at Ebay and send them back to Germany—for three times the price. That's insanity...

SPIEGEL:...and hopefully an exception.

Shikwati: Why do we get these mountains of clothes? No one is freezing here. Instead, our tailors lose their livelihoods. They're in the same position as our farmers. No one in the low-wage world of Africa can be cost-efficient enough to keep pace with donated products. In 1997, 137,000 workers were employed in Nigeria's textile industry. By 2003, the figure had dropped to 57,000. The results are the same in all other areas where overwhelming helpfulness and fragile African markets collide.

> *Why do we get these mountains of clothes? No one is freezing here. Instead, our tailors lose their livelihoods.*

SPIEGEL: Following World War II, Germany only managed to get back on its feet because the Americans poured money into the country through the Marshall Plan. Wouldn't that qualify as successful development aid?

Shikwati: In Germany's case, only the destroyed infrastructure had to be repaired. Despite the economic crisis of the Weimar Republic, Germany was a highly industrialized country before the war. The damages created by the tsunami in Thailand can also be fixed with a little money and some reconstruction aid. Africa, however, must take the first steps into modernity on its own. There must be a change in mentality. We have to stop perceiving ourselves as beggars. These days, Africans perceive themselves only as victims. On the other hand, no one can really picture an African as a businessman. In order to change the current situation, it would be helpful if the aid organizations were to pull out.

> *There must be a change in mentality. We have to stop perceiving ourselves as beggars. These days, Africans perceive themselves only as victims.*

SPIEGEL: If they did that, many jobs would be immediately lost...

Shikwati:...jobs that were created artificially in the first place and that distort reality. Jobs with foreign aid organizations are, of course, quite popular, and they can be very selective in choosing the best people. When an aid organization needs a driver, dozens apply for the job. And because it's unacceptable that the aid worker's chauffeur only speaks his own tribal language, an applicant is needed who also

> *So you end up with some African biochemist driving an aid worker around, distributing European food, and forcing local farmers out of their jobs. That's just crazy!*

Relief and Develop Work

speaks English fluently—and, ideally, one who's also well mannered. So you end up with some African biochemist driving an aid worker around, distributing European food, and forcing local farmers out of their jobs. That's just crazy!

SPIEGEL: The German government takes pride in precisely monitoring the recipients of its funds.

Shikwati: And what's the result? A disaster. The German government threw money right at Rwanda's president Paul Kagame. This is a man who has the deaths of a million people on his conscience—people that his army killed in the neighboring country of Congo.

SPIEGEL: What are the Germans supposed to do?

Shikwati: If they really want to fight poverty, they should completely halt development aid and give Africa the opportunity to ensure its own survival. Currently, Africa is like a child that immediately cries for its babysitter when something goes wrong. Africa should stand on its own two feet.

(Interview conducted by Thilo Thielke; translated from the German by Patrick Kessler, 2005 used with permission)

* * *

In the light of this interview, what are we to do? Do we stop giving as he suggests? Again in the words of the apostle Paul, *may it never be.* We must give. But we must give in a completely different way than the world does.

One of our church members was born in Burundi, Africa, and is currently living and working there. He made this telling statement: "Every time the United Nations comes into a new area, you can just see the brothels pop up all over the place."

What's the difference between church and government agencies? Government agencies pay people to go to places they really don't want to go, and they go there with no moral conviction. Those who voluntarily give up their lives for the sake of Christ have already shown they go with moral conviction.

When the government agencies pull out of a region, there's no one left to continue the work. Whatever was done—is done. There are no means by which to continue the work. This is almost always the case.

Which of the following is better:

(1) A government agency comes in and trains the local people in AIDS awareness. When this agency is gone, all that remains are some pamphlets and some boxes of condoms and, according to Sitaki in the above interview, some very well-paid government officials.

Or:

(2) A Christian agency comes in and trains the church members to minister to AIDS victims and to train volunteers to teach AIDS awareness. When the agency pulls out, the training just keeps going because there are people motivated by love and moral conviction and there's an infrastructure in place to make sure the work continues.

The present leadership in the U.S. government recognizes that faith-based organizations make a lasting and sustainable change, and has chosen as a result to give government funds through these faith-based organizations. It would be foolish not to. It's only the infrastructure of the local church that can sustain the weight of any program for any time.

Unfortunately, not all Christian organizations are committed to working with the local church on the ground. When they pull out of an area, so does any lasting agent of change.

Our church partners with a relief agency in Central Africa. One of the best compliments they ever received is a statement I personally heard a church volunteer make regarding their work in Rwanda: "Other agencies have come in, done their thing, and then left. When they leave, so does all the work they did. You guys come in, teach us, and when you leave—we just keep doing it."

Relief and development work cannot afford to be content with anything less than this.

Relief or Development?

There will always be a need to respond to disasters by providing relief, including food, medicine, temporary shelters, and clothing. And we should be generous when we see such misery. But something is wrong if we're so short-sighted that we do nothing to try to prevent these situations in the first place.

- Is it better to clean up after an earthquake, or to teach the local people to build in such a way as to withstand an earthquake?

- Is it better to prevent a famine, or to give away food after the fact?

- Is it better to feed the starving, or to teach them to feed themselves?

- Is a temporary fix better, or a permanent one?

- Is it better to train teachers, or to come in and teach kids one week a year?

- Is it better to train communities in hygiene and health care, or to provide medicine once they're sick?

If the answer to these questions are obvious—and they are—then we shouldn't be merely waiting around to respond to disasters. As believers, we should be involved in development.

Anytime we give to help the suffering of those who are destitute, this is good. But the question is, "Is there a better way to give?" And ultimately it should be our goal to give in the best way possible.

Here again, it's good to apply the four principles—*relationship, accountability, indigenous sustainability,* and *equity.*

Relationship: Ask yourself these questions: Can I go? Can a team from my church go? In any disaster, bodies are needed to help do the work. Money spent to send people is money well spent. Not only do our church members meet practical needs when we send them, but their lives are changed as well.

Which church or churches can we partner with? Chances are, the local churches are already mobilizing. Unlike big government agencies, local churches know the needs of their people and how to meet them.

> *Money spent to send people is money well spent.*

In the recent hurricane Katrina disaster, many victims commented that the local church was the most helpful agency. By partnering with the church at the site of the disaster, the unity of the body is put into practice, the name of Christ is lifted up as it should be, and real physical and spiritual needs are met.

Accountability: If a relationship exists beyond a purely financial agreement with a local church, there's already a natural accountability built into the relationship. It's always best to go in person, but if you're not able to go, give through an agency which partners with local churches.

Indigenous sustainability: Working with the local church empowers them and provides a natural means for continued follow-up when we need to leave. The locals will be more effective in judging whether or not those soliciting help are taking advantage of them, or coming for help due to a legitimate need. By working through the local church in a given area, we empower this church, and their presence and impact will continue to be there long after we're gone. They're also the ones who have the relationship with the local people around them, so it's not nearly so likely they'll be taken advantage of like foreigners often are.

> *Unlike big government agencies, local churches know the needs of their people and how to meet them.*

Equity: In a disaster, the church has a unique opportunity to be a true light to all who are perishing. All people in the vicinity of the church should be reached out to regardless of race or religion.

The Old Testament continually talks about taking care of the widow, the orphan, and the refugee/alien (who in the Old Testament was obviously from another people and religion).

Cross-Cultural Relief and Development

Cross-cultural disaster relief requires an extra element that's often overlooked. A disaster like Katrina that occurs within the confines of our own culture makes is possible to directly link up with a church on the ground in the area of that disaster. We understand the culture, the language, the economics, and the systems of accounting. But when a church in America tries to directly partner

GIVING WISELY?

with a church in the third world without cultural understanding, we can create all kinds of inequities. We don't understand the cultural systems for accountability and what it means to create something that's sustainable. Cultural expertise is needed if cross-cultural relief and development efforts are going to be truly productive.

It's indeed best for the American church to work with local churches in cross-cultural settings, but it needs to be done through an expert who understands these two things: (1) He or she must understand the different cultures of the churches seeking to work together. (2) He or she must understand sustainable and empowering relief and development work, and the power of money to both help and destroy.

How to Choose a Relief Organization

When choosing which relief and development organization to give through, make sure they're about empowering the local churches on the ground to do the work and aren't simply doing it themselves. It's often easier to bypass the local churches already there on the ground, and many Christian relief organizations do, but this isn't the way to bring lasting change. Not only does working with the local church show an organization's desire to bring about sustainable change, but by doing so, this brings glory to God by bringing glory to his bride—the church.

Also make sure they're willing to work with churches here on this side of the ocean. Partnerships should go both ways—you must get people from your church involved in building the relationships with both the agency and the local church where you're working.

A good relief organization works with every church in an undeveloped area that's willing to do the work, so it's important for us as western churches not to demand that we work with a single

It's often easier to bypass the local churches on the ground, and many Christian relief organizations do, but this isn't the way to bring lasting change.

church. Exclusively partnering with a single church can create inequities in a region and get the local churches jealous of each other. A good agency can help our churches be aware of this kind of thing.

A good agency can also educate on what kind of giving is good, and what kind is harmful.

Remember *RAISE—Relationship, Accountability, Indigenous Sustainability* (through empowering the local church), and *Equity*. An organization that's all about these things is a good one to support.

The Incredible Gift of a Loan

He who is kind to the poor lends to the LORD;
God will reward him for what he has done.
(Hebrew Proverb)

The Scriptures tell us to give without thought of return. So the thought of giving a loan to someone and expecting him or her to pay it back—and then to have the gall to call such an act "generosity"—seems incredibly wrong. But in fact, a loan is perhaps the best gift we can give to help out those suffering in the third world.

If I give a poor family in Sudan a gift of a hundred dollars, they'll likely run out and buy the food and clothing they've been longing for. In a few days the hundred dollars will be gone, and there will be no lasting change taking its place.

If however I give a loan to this same family, requiring them to

GIVING WISELY?

pay it back within a two-month time span, this would force the family to think about starting a business that could generate more income than the loan itself. The family invests the money, starts a small business and makes $150. They pay back $100, and make $50 dollars a month for the next two years. The $100 is reinvested in another family.

It's truly a gift that keeps on giving.

Bankers can't be bothered with such pitifully small loans, but many relief organizations have started such microfinance institutions because of their remarkable ability to help people lift themselves out of the cycle of poverty. Some of the better institutions have over a 98 percent payback rate because of the communal nature of the loan and the peer pressure to pay back these loans. To give the capital necessary to start these institutions is perhaps one of the best ways to make sure your gift will be used over and over again. It's a way to use your gift of cash to lift hundreds out of the cycle of poverty they've found themselves in.

Our church has taken offerings to get these institutions started, and I've been on the high mountaintops of Rwanda talking with widows and mothers of small children whose lives have been changed by these gifts. The gifts were hard, in the sense that work had to be done to make it pay, but believe me, these women thanked me and my church with songs and stories of gratitude because we'd invested in their community. Our church gave a gift and it was the gift of a loan. It's never transformational to undermine an economy, but it's life-transforming if our giving can actually create an economy.

Chapter Fourteen

Training and Education
Is the West the Best?

Understanding is vastly superior to
knowledge.

A PROVERB SOMEWHERE, SOMETIME, PROBABLY — WELL, MAYBE

Wisdom is supreme; therefore get wisdom.
Though it cost all you have, get
understanding.

HEBREW PROVERB

China, 1986: Wang Quan (not real name) had never met a Christian believer in his life. But his heart hungered for God.

Life for a young man in China who aspires to go to college is filled with stress we cannot even imagine here in the West. In the stress of these years, Wang prayed to God for supernatural help on an exam he felt he might not be able to pass, and the fear of not passing, and what that would mean for his future, literally terrified him.

God heard Wang Quan's prayer, and he was certain it was God, for he scored higher on the test than those he knew to be much smarter and better prepared than he had been.

Being now convinced of the reality of God in a land where he'd been taught nothing but the atheism of a Marxist Communist system, he cried out for God to show him the truth and the right way to live.

The next day he saw a foreigner walking down the street with a cross around his neck. "Can you tell me about God?" Wang Quan asked the foreigner in his broken English.

This man he'd approached was a visiting scholar. He was a Yugoslavian who was teaching the Hittite language to Chinese students using German textbooks while teaching the class in English. The conspicuous cross around his neck was one he'd bought from a Navajo reservation while visiting the United States. It was huge, and made of silver, turquoise, and red coral. The unfortunate thing was that this man, Sylvan, could tell him nothing of God. The cross was merely a "cool" decoration. But Sylvan knew some Christians in the city, and being a kind man, he took Wang Quan back to his guesthouse and introduced him to some of these believers who lived near him.

That was when I first met Wang Quan. An amazing guy. He grew by leaps and bounds in his faith, and immediately began sharing his faith with his girlfriend who was a member of the communist party. They agreed to have a debate. If he won, she would become a Christian; if she won, he agreed to become a Communist party member. Well, he won.

I was privileged to witness this extraordinary couple grow in their relationship with God as one of my teammates worked with them and taught them about their new found faith.

> They agreed to have a debate. If he won, she would become a Christian; if she won, he agreed to become a Communist party member.

Wang Quan was hungry for God, extraordinarily gifted, and

loved the English language. He had such a heart for his people and even shared his faith with the North Koreans who were studying on his campus. He decided that he wanted to reach North Koreans for Christ—and being Chinese, he could reach both Chinese and North Koreans in China. He also hoped to eventually travel to North Korea. But he really felt the need to be trained biblically first.

There was one problem: Undergraduates were never, under any circumstance, allowed to leave China.

China had one open seminary at the time, and it was very liberal in its theology. He started looking into schools elsewhere. He was accepted at a Christian school in the United States. There was one problem: Undergraduates were never, under any circumstance, allowed to leave China. Unless, of course, someone's praying. So through a series of miraculous events, Wang Quan found himself with only one remaining obstacle to leaving China: the American Embassy.

At the Embassy, the official who controlled Wang Quan's destiny said sternly, "You've got permission from your government to go abroad as an undergrad. I haven't seen this before. Why do you want to go to the United States?"

"To tell you the truth, I want to learn the Bible so I can be an evangelist and reach my country and the North Koreans with the gospel." The official miraculously approved his visa.

Relationships with Americans funded his way, and Wang left China as an undergrad (which simply never happens) to go to America to study the Bible at a Christian school. He was destined to become the first Chinese evangelist to the North Koreans, and Americans were eager to pay his way through school to get him back on the field as soon as possible.

That was twenty-one years ago. And where is Wang Quan now? Still in the U.S. He has kids just finishing high school who are full-blooded Americans. He got married just before he left China, and again through some incredible events, his wife was able to join him in America. But after having two children—which isn't allowed in China—it became very impractical to go back. So here they reside. America has two more well-trained Christians.

Wang Quan isn't the exception—he's the rule. Most students who are sponsored to come to the U.S. so they can go back to help their people end up staying here. It was totally Wang Quan's intention to only be here for a time. I don't doubt the intention of most of these faith-filled youth. But America exerts its hold on them, and will not easily let go.

I don't blame Wang Quan for staying in the U.S. The U.S is a great place to live. In fact, I'm now living here. So I can't blame him in the least. But there's a sense of loss that one of China's brightest hopes for China and North Korea got side-tracked.

Was it wrong to bring Wang Quan to the United States? No. What's wrong is expecting him to go back. Whenever we bring a foreign student to the United States, we should look at it as "immigration"—not as a step to equip him to minister to his own culture.

Was it wrong to bring him to the United States? No. What's wrong is expecting him to go back.

And if someone like Wang Quan does take that huge step of faith to go back home, it's very wrong for us to expect him to fit in once he does go back.

Think about it. An African man comes to the United States to get his PhD. This means he's going to be in the States for some six to ten years. He leaves his small one-room mud house with a grass roof and dirt floor and no electricity, and he steps into an American apartment. His new American church feels bad that his family isn't here with him, so they volunteer to pay for them to come—and then they need a house. We feel guilty when we see them all living in a small place, and it's illegal (in some states) for his boy and girl who are older than ten to be in the same room. So the church helps him into a typical American home, and his church showers him with all the American "necessities"—sofas, microwaves, a television, and other things he'd never seen before, but now quickly gets used to. His kids start American schools which are quite a bit different from the ones with mud walls, a tin roof, and a hundred kids packed into one room—like they were back home.

After living here for six to ten years, his kids have become Americans through and through. Are they going to want to give up the dreams implanted in this new culture of cash, cars, college, and careers, and go back to Africa and live in a one-room hut? The chances are slim.

This family has been fundamentally changed at its very core. If they do go back to their home country, there's no hope of a good college, they no longer dress or think like the African kids they once were, and they now have nothing in common with them. After all, their kids are now essentially American. The man and his wife have learned a different lifestyle dependent upon all the latest technology. What was essential for life before coming to America and what's considered essential now are two totally different things. This family may never be fully American, but they certainly will never be fully African again.

There's nothing inherently wrong with this—it's just a fact.

Our church supports a man from a developing country who'd been brought here to do his doctoral work. Upon finishing, he bravely has gone back to his home country. He just sent us his financial needs for the year—$21,000. American missionaries in that country require about twice that. The average national pastor in his country makes about one fifteenth of that—or about $1,500 a year. Someone with the equivalent degree and equivalent position at a university from that country would make about $5,000—one fourth of our friend's needs.

These financial needs reflect the fact that this family, upon returning to Africa, really is between two worlds. The locals see them as a family that's sort of local, and they love and respect them —they speak the local language, and know the customs—but they live a lot like the other Americans around with kids back in the United States working and going to college, and with a house that looks like a hybrid of a local home and an American home.

So this family is somewhere in between. Now that's not bad. It's just a fact.

There's a simple rule: *If you want a person to reach his or her own culture, don't take him out of it.* Don't take someone out of a relatively impoverished country, show him the glitter and comfort and material excess of the U.S., and then expect him to want to go back. Don't take a Chinese man from China, train him in a western school and American mega-church ministry techniques, and then expect him to slip back into his culture like he'd never left. Don't expect this man to take his kids

> *There's a simple rule: If you want a person to reach his or her own culture, don't take him out of it.*

out of a great American educational system and go back to his own country where there's virtually no educational system.

Is the best use of our money to pay for a student's education, green card, and eventual American citizenship? Sure, if that's our goal. But if our goal is to train the local believer to reach the people around him, it's not at all cost-effective, and educationally very inappropriate to rip someone out of their culture and train them in the materialistic environment and in the ways of the West. It's no wonder that, according to an academic dean at a leading biblical seminary, over 80 percent of those who come to study never return to live in their home country. The percentages are higher for those studying business or other skills when their home country's economy has a place for them. But the percentage who stay is still extremely high.

I've seen some short-term study programs that are very successful. Some subjects (in the business or medical field) can be learned only in developed countries. Programs of one term or less have a very high return rate. Just remember—the longer someone stays abroad in school, the less likely they'll return. There's a direct correlation.

This, of course, doesn't mean we should not educate or train. Americans are so well trained and educated, and we have so much to offer. So what option do we have? If we don't bring them here, what then?

Build and support traditional seminaries in their culture? Traditional seminaries are institutions that take the student out of the environment of their world. There they live, eat, and learn at the institution. Then after several years they graduate and step out and back into their world to minister. This is much better than taking someone far off to America. It's without question a step in the right direction.

The traditional seminary is good, and there are many international institutions that are doing a great job of training the locals on their native turf or at least closer to it. Many of these schools need scholars to come and teach. They're a good way to instruct locals and to keep them in or close to their native culture. Many are worthy of our support, and the training and resources we can offer them.

But is there a better way?

I don't believe the traditional model is best for all cultures for a couple of reasons. One, it's a relatively recent cultural product of the West. And two, it's often the case that learning in this environment takes place apart from any substantial culturally relevant application.

A New Kind of Training

In recent years a new model for biblical education has surfaced that I believe to be superior to the traditional seminary in many respects. It not only allows a person to stay within his own culture, but it allows him to stay in his own ministry in his own village. Instead of removing people from ministry for several years—filling their heads with knowledge—and sending them back, this model keeps them ministering and using all they learn along the way to empower others.

> *Instead of removing people from ministry for several years—filling their heads with knowledge—and sending them back, this model keeps them ministering and using all they learn along the way to empower others.*

There are different ways for this to work, but one that I've observed is called the Periodic Model. In this model, the year is broken into three periods of four months each. In each period, the students leave their home for only a month at a time. They're trained with solid biblical teaching; then they go back home for the remaining three months of the period, where they continue ministry in their church. They're required to teach twelve others the things they've just learned. When the next period comes and they're gone for another one-month training session, those they've just trained are expected to do their share of the ministry back home.

Anyone who has ever been required to teach knows that this is perhaps the greatest way to learn. Application is constant, learning from teaching is increased, and the local culture is reached, all at the same time—three things conspicuously missing from the traditional seminary approach.

I'm firmly committed to sound biblical teaching, and therefore our church has partnered with schools like these.

How does this model do in terms of the RAISE principles?

Relationship: This model is extremely relational. It bears fruit in the lives of those who are studying in the "one month in, three months out" seminaries. It also bears fruit in the lives of the pastors and theologically trained teachers whom we send to teach the nationals. It's a wonderful privilege for us to spend time with people of great faith such as those we get to teach and train. We come back with more than we were able to give. The lives of our pastors and the theologically trained who go to train the nationals are forever impacted. It's such a blessing to rub up against the lives and hearts of the ones we go to train.

Accountability: Money can be used in an accountable fashion.

Indigenous sustainability: This teaching empowers people to teach and train others, which is the seed that stands the greatest chance of producing complete indigenous sustainability. This kind of education can continue even if foreigners are kicked out. It allows as much teaching as possible to come from those of their own culture.

Equity: These schools don't take the person out of their host culture, and they allow them to live at the same standard they've been accustomed to, and at the standard of those to whom they're ministering.

The Power of Books

Good books are empowering and really never create dependency. Getting good Christian books into the hands of local leaders is one of the best ways we can help.

A friend of mine who's a Christian writer gives his books away by the thousands to national pastors and ministers of the gospel. Suddenly an untrained man has months of teaching material that he would never have had apart from the larger body of Christ.

Books often sit on our shelves at home. But when a book falls into the hands of a local believer in the third world who has no access to bookstores, it is read and read and read. It's by far a better gift than our gold. Getting whole libraries into the hands of schools, seminaries, and churches that will last and be used for years to come is a gift that keeps on giving. The believer and the community are both truly empowered.

Chapter Fifteen

First-Rate Local Giving

Helping to Restore God's Image in Our Community

He raises the poor up from the dust and lifts
the needy from the ash heap; He seats them
with royalty, with the princes of their people.

KING DAVID

Do not conform any longer to the ways of this
world, but be transformed by the renewing of
your mind.

PAUL THE APOSTLE

Our giving should work to accomplish two related objectives.

1. to show the compassion of Christ.

2. to truly help the person who's in need.

If our giving doesn't truly help the person and does nothing to meet their deepest need, then how does this show the compassion of Christ? How can our money be used to meet the deepest needs of those around us? We need to redefine what it means to be compassionate.

> If a brother or sister is without clothing and in need of daily food, and one of you says to them, "Go in peace, be warmed and be filled," and yet you do not give them what's necessary for their body, what use is that? (James 2:15-16)

If we don't respond in such circumstances, how is the compassion of Christ seen? James says it simply is not. We must respond to the needs of those in our community, but how?

We as Christians, and most churches, have developed a reputation for being compassionate, which is good; unfortunately we've also developed a reputation for being extremely easy to take advantage of. Churches all over the nation

We as Christians, and most churches, have developed a reputation for being extremely easy to take advantage of.

are being exposed to a new kind of beggar—one who has learned to take advantage of such blind generosity.

Here's a common scenario:

A guy drops into the church office. By the smell and appearance of the guy, you can tell he's been down on his luck. "Hey," he says, "I've got a real problem. I was wondering if there's any way your church could help me out."

"Maybe we can. What's the problem?"

"Well, the wife and kids and I have hit some really hard times. I lost my job, got into some trouble. A lot of it's my own fault. We moved up here a couple of years ago to try to make a go of it, and now it has all fallen apart. I called my old employer back in my hometown, and he has offered me my old job back. The only problem is, I'm out of gas and don't have enough money to get me back home. If I could just get enough to fill my tank, I sure would be appreciative."

So what do you do? To say no seems cruel and heartless and flies in the face of everything James talks about. Yet to give him fifty dollars and send him on his way—when this might be some kind of scam—seems naïve at best.

Some suggest, "Just give it to him. God will hold this man accountable for his actions, just as he'll hold us responsible for our action of either giving or withholding."

To allow a guy to walk the paths of lies, then go and pay him to do it, is to purchase this guy's one way ticket to Hades. It's a serious sin against the man. Can this rightly be called compassion?

I want to suggest that to just give him the money and send him on his way is perhaps not the compassionate thing to do at all. It's the easy thing, yes. But true compassion is rarely as easy as handing someone some cash and sending him on his way.

Let's just suppose that this guy is lying, like most people with such stories are indeed found to be. Is it compassionate to reward a lie with a large wad of cash? Or is the most compassionate thing to confront him in his lie and then contact all the churches in the area to make sure none of them let him get away with lying as well? To allow a guy to walk the path of lies, then go and pay him to do it, is to purchase his one way ticket to Hades. It's a serious sin against the man. Can this rightly be called compassion?

The very last words of the book of James scream at us here:

> My brethren, if any among you strays from the truth and one turns him back, let him know that he who turns a sinner from the error of his way will save his soul from death and will cover a multitude of sins.

Also, to encourage a man who's able to work—in a land where

work is available—to simply live the life of a beggar by taking advantage of people isn't in any way good or compassionate.

The goal of all compassion should be restorative. True compassion doesn't wish a life of lies, deceit and idleness upon anyone. To wish such anti-virtues upon anyone can truly be seen only as hate—which simply put is the desire for another's destruction. Now, if the way we're responding to people who come into our church is pushing them further and further down this road of destruction, then we're not being compassionate at all. We're only *feeling* compassionate in our act of giving—but feeling compassion and showing compassion are two different things. God calls us to do both.

> *The goal of all compassion should be restorative.*

The compassionate road is not the easy one. The easy way is to "hand them a fifty" and hope they make it back home. The compassionate road is the one that does all it can to make sure they truly get back home. This means spiritually as well.

Look at the story of the Good Samaritan in Luke 10. It wasn't the easy road. The first thing the Scriptures say about the Samaritan was that when he saw the injured man, "he felt compassion." We know this was real compassion because of what followed. "He came to him, bandaged his wounds, pouring oil and wine on them." Time and effort. This man sacrificed his own time, his own goods, and his own energy because of the need he saw.

Imagine if the Samaritan had seen this great need—the man lying battered and bruised and lying there to die—and the passage said, "He felt compassion on him, and so he took some gold coins and laid them on the road beside the injured man."

We've must first realize that when people come into our church for help, we, more often than not, are dealing with those who have been battered and bruised and who are laying beside the road. It's true that they may be asking for money, but their problems are never solved that simply. If it's truly a financial need, their need is still almost always greater than just money. If it's a scam and a liar who's trying to take advantage of the church, "how much greater this man's injuries must be." But with either person, if we respond with cash only, we haven't truly been compassionate.

If we respond with cash only, we haven't truly been compassionate.

> "But a Samaritan, who was on a journey, came upon him; and when he saw him, he felt compassion, and came to him and bandaged up his wounds, pouring oil and wine on them; and he put him on his own beast, and brought him to an inn and took care of him.
>
> "On the next day he took out two denarii and gave them to the innkeeper and said, 'Take care of him; and whatever more you spend, when I return I will repay you.'
>
> "Which of these three do you think proved to be a neighbor to the man who fell into the robbers' hands?"
>
> And he said, "The one who showed mercy toward him."
>
> Then Jesus said to him, "Go and do the same." (Luke 10:33-37)

This Samaritan did what he could, then paid someone even better equipped than himself to take care of the injured man. The hero of the story gave much of his time, money, and other resources, but what's interesting is that he didn't give any money to the victim. Now that's not saying it would have been wrong to do so. But true compassion—of the very highest kind—can be accomplished without giving any money at all directly to the victim. This goes against so much of what we've been taught. Compassionate giving is so much more than writing a check, or handing someone a few bucks.

> *But true compassion—of the very highest kind—can be accomplished without giving any money at all directly to the victim.*

God wants His people involved in the ministry of redeeming and transforming lives, not merely giving cash. It's when we get involved in the game that our lives are truly transformed. It's the kind of difference between those who pay handsomely to sit and watch the Rose Bowl from row 67 and those who are down on the field playing for the national championship. Those in row 67 have not been pruned and shaped and formed into the image of football players. God calls us all to be on the field, not to simply buy tickets. It's when we're on the field that we're conformed to the image of Christ.

We need to invest ourselves in the problems, and not merely our money. Yes, it's true that our money is indeed part of us, and when we invest ourselves that includes our money. But it's equally true that we can be guilty of substituting money for ourselves, and therefore we're not allowing God to work His change in us. We are called to get out of the grandstands and into the game – not to simply buy a ticket and watch others.

The goal of the Samaritan was restoration. In compassion he saw the need, and he did not provide for the guy while he was in the ditch, but got him out of the ditch and restored him to health. This meant that for a time the needs of the injured man would be taken care of for him -because he was incapacitated - but this was never the end goal. The goal was restoration.

All churches need to have a plan of restoration. Churches need

First-Rate Local Giving

people who can provide life coaching and others who are trained to take in families for a time, so as to get them on their feet again. Still others need to know how to find out who's lying to them about their needs so these lies can be confronted. If a person simply wants to be kept alive in the ditch by the side of the road—the government is good at doing that. The church needs to be about transformation and restoration.

If there's a family that has to be constantly bailed out by the church, the church needs to do something more. Money can be the thing that feeds this problem of dependency. A man who cannot provide for his household needs to be taught how to do so. If he refuses to be taught, he shouldn't be rewarded monetarily for such a refusal.

Granted, there are those who are mentally handicapped, or widows who cannot work. Paul said such people should be put on the list. But to those who are young and capable Paul said, "Get them to work. Allow them to come to understand what it means to be created in the image of God. Give them the dignity that only work and providing for one's own can provide."

Giving to Support Yourself?

Why does "support yourself" sound strange to us?

Well, that's simple enough. By definition, giving is to *others,* not to yourself. Giving to yourself isn't giving at all. Or can it be?

Jenni had a dream. She wanted to go to Russia so she could help, live, and serve in an orphanage there. She'd been there for a couple weeks one summer and found herself compelled to go back to see these kids reached with the love of Jesus.

She did something extremely unusual by today's mission modes. She first went to Alaska to work her tail off so she could earn enough money to go to Russia to live for a year. She worked in unbelievable conditions that no comfortable white American could endure. She worked with almost all Filipinos. The other white Americans quit after a few days or weeks because the work was just too hard. But Jenni endured and saved the money she earned from cutting and packing fish. God used her greatly in the lives of the Filipinos as she worked side by side with them, sixteen to eighteen hours a day.

She then did something extremely selfish. She spent that money on her own dream. She sent herself to Russia to work at the orphanage for a year.

Wait! I can hear your objection. That is not selfish! You're right.

Often one of the most generous ways we can give of our money is to empower ourselves to do that which God has created and gifted us to do. I've found, however, many feel guilty about doing this very thing. It's not really giving unless it goes to the church or to missions or to the needy. Well, you are the church, or you're at least a significant part of it, and God has created you for a mission and to go to the needy.

Which will do more good for God's kingdom: (1) You put five dollars in an offering for the homeless downtown. (2) You decide to take that five dollars to go downtown to the homeless shelter where you spend the whole day loving on and listening to people who never have known love.

Just this last weekend I took my wife and kids and their friends downtown to a ministry that doesn't just feed the homeless,

First-Rate Local Giving

but involves folks like me so we can engage these dear people in relationship. My wife, son, and I spent an hour and a half talking to two guys—Kevin, who was sleeping each night under the Glisan Street Bridge, and Jason, who was living in his car. We simply asked questions and listened. Guess who showed up at our church that Sunday, some 26 miles away? And they weren't asking for anything. They just wanted to go where they were loved. Relationship is the beginning of real transformation. Six dollars of gas money bought my family relationship with these guys. It was the most rewarding investment I'd made in a long time.

Are you gifted in hospitality? What good is it if you give all your money away for another to do missions, so you're left completely devoid of resources to have needy people into your home to live for a time so you can help shepherd and counsel them?

Budget Money to Give Toward Your Mission

So what is your mission? Where has God gifted you to serve—meeting the needs of the many around you?

When you sit down and decide to sacrificially give, don't forget to make sure you're able to give toward your calling. Of course, you could abuse this and say you need a brand new Victorian sofa so you can be hospitable. Actually such a sofa might discourage hospitality because you wouldn't want anyone to spill on it. So be careful you aren't deluding yourself and using this as an excuse.

My wife puts money into our budget to buy books to give away. We also budget money to be hospitable and to let families who are in trouble live with us for a time while we and our church work with them to get them standing on their own feet again. Money spent like this is no less giving than if we'd put it in the offering plate. In fact, this money empowers us to exercise our gifts for ministry.

It's true—there's no tax deduction for such giving—at least this side of heaven.

What's the goal here? One of the reasons we're so confused when it comes down to deciding how we give is that we forget the goal. When someone comes to our church asking for a handout, and I have no objective in mind but to be nice, there's no way for me to decide what to do.

The Goal Is Total Transformation—Don't Settle for Less

> Let him who steals steal no longer, but rather let him labor, performing with his own hands what is good, in order that he may have something to share with him who has need. (Ephesians 4:28)

This passage is talking about someone who's stealing to make a living. It's about the transformation of a thief into a man who gives to make a difference in the lives of others. It's about total transformation. This is the business of the church.

A dear family in our church had four kids of their own and three foster kids. Then the family took in another child for a year. This family, which now numbered ten, was all nicely packed into a three-bedroom house. Their hearts were big, but they weren't able to make ends meet financially. So where did they go for help? To the church—of course. But it was going not to the church just once. It was regularly. They were coming almost monthly to get enough money to pay the bills. My wife, who was good friends with the woman, decided to broach the subject with her.

"But *, you don't want to have to keep taking from the church every month."

"But Janie," came her quick reply, "that's what the church is for —to help meet people's needs."

Wow. What do you say to that? That's what the church is for. Right?

Yes, but "help meet people's needs" to what end? So they'll keep coming week after week with more needs? So they'll learn the satisfaction of being dependent on others in place of the God given satisfaction of knowing that you're caring for your own—and giving to others who are in need? We as individuals and churches must answer no.

We're to give, yes. But not necessarily in the way the person is asking us to. Not when it falls desperately short of meeting the person's deepest need.

A person's greatest need is to be transformed by the grace of God in a relationship with Jesus so they can grow to a place where they can become someone who gives. We were created to give. We're doing what we were created in the image of God to do when we give. Someone who's dependent on another is not in a position to give. They need to be empowered and transformed and placed in that position. God's church—the body of Christ—is to be that agent of change. The problem is, it's so much easier to simply give money than it is to be about transformation.

Listen to how difficult Paul made it for people—and not just people, but widows—to get permanent help from the church:

> Honor widows who are widows indeed; but if any widow has children or grandchildren, they must first learn to practice piety in regard to their own family and to make some return to their parents; for this is acceptable in the sight of God. Now she who is a widow indeed and who has been left alone, has fixed her hope on God and continues in entreaties and prayers night and day. But she who gives herself to wanton pleasure is dead even while she lives. Prescribe these things as well, so that they may be above reproach. But if anyone does not provide for his own, and especially for those of his household, he has denied the faith and is worse than an unbeliever. (1 Timothy 5:3-8)

This is an incredibly strong statement. Paul offers no excuse for a believer to not be taking care of his own. We as churches and individuals should never give an excuse for them to remain in such a sorry state by the way we give money. If a man has a job that doesn't provide enough, we don't make up the difference—instead we must either help him find the job that will provide, or we get him into a place where he can live within his means.

> A widow is to be put on the list only if she is not less than sixty years old, having been the wife of one man, having a reputation for good works; and if she has brought up children, if she has shown hospitality to strangers, if she has washed the saints' feet, if she has assisted those in distress, and if she has devoted herself to every good work. (1 Timothy 5:9-10)

Paul even has moral qualifications in order to be on the list. This seems opposed to so much of what we think today about giving without strings attached. The unconditional love approach to

The unconditional love approach to giving is not biblical. The tough love approach is the biblical model here.

First-Rate Local Giving

giving is not biblical. The tough love approach is the biblical model here.

> But refuse to put younger widows on the list, for when they feel sensual desires in disregard of Christ, they want to get married, thus incurring condemnation, because they have set aside their previous pledge. At the same time they also learn to be idle, as they go around from house to house; and not merely idle, but also gossips and busybodies, talking about things not proper to mention. (1Timothy 5:11-13)

Our giving can actually teach people to be idle. This was the problem Paul was reacting to. Our giving should produce fruit and transform people. It should not create or allow for a life of idleness and gossip.

> Therefore, I want younger widows to get married, bear children, keep house, and give the enemy no occasion for reproach; for some have already turned aside to follow Satan. If any woman who is a believer has dependent widows, she must assist them and the church must not be burdened, so that it may assist those who are widows indeed. (1Timothy 5:14-16)

Paul was concerned about there being an unnecessary burden on the church. Helping to transform someone who needs into someone who gives and invests in others is actually not giving but investing. There's real return for the money in these lives. We're to *invest* in people, not merely give to them. Mere giving is burdensome and cripples those who we're pretending to help. Investing in transformation brings life and empowers the giver as well as the one who receives.

We're to invest in people, not merely give to them.

Imagine the following all-too-real scenario: A family comes to the church in crisis and asks for financial assistance. Which is easier to do:

(A) Give them the thousand dollars they ask for that keeps them from being evicted, and be done with them (for at least a month).

(B) Provide the spiritual counseling, the financial counseling, the career counseling, the marital counseling, the drug rehabilitation program, etc. that they really need to get back on their feet, in right standing with God and with each other, so as to bring them to a place where they can give freely to others in need.

Option A is so much easier to accomplish, and granted, the family coming in for assistance may not even want the B option. And frankly, most churches are not even in a place where they can offer option B.

So because A is the easy and doable option, this is the route we often take. But there's only one problem. A is the simply the wrong option.

It's the duty of the church to do the right thing. It's our duty to be about transforming lives. Option B is the right option. And the church must put people in places where we can be about really helping people. As long as churches are settling for the easy option, Option A, the family in need will also go for this option and there will never be any life change; they'll never be transformed. The love of Jesus which works its way out through His bride, the church, is about transformation. It's not the easy road, but we cannot afford to settle for less.

> *As long as churches are settling for the easy option, the family in need will also always go for this easy option and there will never be any life change; they will never be transformed.*

Talk about taking the tough road—I just received a letter in the mail of someone asking for help. Real help. Included is the letter and my appeal to our congregation to answer it.

GIVING WISELY?

Hello!

I realize you don't know me, but my name is John Hansel (not real name). And you've been a part of my family's life for several years through the prison's Angel Tree project and I would like to thank you on behalf of my children, Robert & Alexandra and myself.

My next question is that I'm about ready to be released back in the community on 5.15.2009.

I have limited resources and have lost contact with a majority of my family in the last three years. I've been in prison since 1998 for drug & delivery related charges.

You wouldn't happen to have any type of resources, or a program that you could refer me too?

Once again, I would like to thank you for taking the time to read this letter.

Sincerely,
John
(OSP)
Salem, Oregon

My appeal to our church body for a response:

Amazing letter. This man has been led to the living water by our body's love in action. A drug dealer. In the pen for ten years. I looked at the return address. O.S.P. It took me awhile. Oregon State Penitentiary. Scary.

Can we...do we dare take someone like this in? Do we have systems in place to help someone like this find his place in the community?

Maybe a better question is this: If we — the church — can't help him, who can? So what are we going to do?

He will need a job — or going back to selling drugs may be his only option. But who will risk giving this man a job? Will you?

He will need fellowship. But what small group is willing to risk taking him in?

He will need discipleship. Who will spend an hour or two a week with him? Starting now by going to visit him in the penitentiary?

His kids need mentors in their lives' right now. Who will take them out to Starbucks once a week for a strawberry cappuccino? Who will take James fishing? Who will teach Victoria to do crafts? Who will take them to church when Mom has to work?

Through the Angel Tree gift program Timothy has been lead to the love we have here at this church — and now he has written looking for hope. But that hope only can be as deep as our love for him. How deep does our love go?

I know the answer: "For I am convinced that neither death nor life, nor angels nor principalities, nor things present nor things to come, no powers...no height nor depth, nor any other created thing shall be able to separate us from the love of Christ."

This is the kind of love that is around this place. It is the kind of love that will step into danger and say, "The Lord is with me." It is the kind that reaches into the dirt and is not afraid of getting dirty. It is in these unclean places that Jesus spent his ministry years. He ministered in these places simply because it is in these places that people are most keenly aware of their need for a Savior.

Timothy Hassel has a need. Let's rise to the occasion, get radical, and meet it. He has been lead to the water by our kind actions. Now let us chose to let him drink. Let us not only be known for a cup of cold water — but as a spring of life — a fountain that bubbles over.

The afflicted and needy are seeking water, but there is none,
And their tongue is parched with thirst;
I, the LORD, will answer them Myself,
As the God of Israel I will not forsake them. (Isaiah 41:17)

Jonathan

We as churches must ask the question: Are we in a position to really help hurting people? To see real transformation? If the answer is no, it's not about giving more money, it's about using our money and training our people to get these systems in place. It's about finding those organizations in the community that are already doing these things well and getting our people and money behind them.

To be effective in transforming lives and families stuck in the cycle of dependency every church needs to have people or systems in place that can provide the following:

- *Financial classes and budget coaching*: So many money problems are simply cured by teaching people how to not spend more than they have. Every church should have some means of teaching these things. To take someone who's in debt and to see them changed into someone who gives to make a difference in the lives of others and for God's kingdom — this is transformation. Churches need to have some system in place to help bring about this kind of change.

- *Career counseling and coaching*: Many men and women simply need to know what it is they can do to provide for their family. They need to be pointed in the right direction.

- *Marital and family counseling*: Some financial issues are purely symptoms of a much greater problem at home. Whoever is receiving temporary financial assistance from the church often is in even greater need of this kind of help. The real underlying problems of a family must be addressed.

- *Job interview training*: Someone can simply help those in need know how to interview for a job. This is a small thing, but huge in its impact. This can be done merely by providing the right video or book, but can make the difference of tens of thousands of dollars of income a year for a family.

- *Real Christian discipleship*: An individual must be willing to really grow in his walk with God. Any of the above without this taking place is a band-aid solution at best. Real lasting transformation is one of the heart.

A church without these five things in place is not in a position to truly help the needy around them. We need to invest to get these systems in place. To give money to the needy without speaking to these basic needs is perhaps even more harmful than throwing our money away. Such giving only gives the appearance of generosity and fails to make any real and lasting difference—whether in this life or in the one to come. To meet these needs is showing the real transformational compassion of Christ and meeting true human needs.

> *To give money to the needy without speaking to these basic needs is perhaps even more harmful than throwing our money away.*

First-Rate Principles for Giving Locally
(A Local Adaptation of the RAISE Principles)

So, in summing up, think of *RATE* — Relationship, Accountability, Transformation, Equity.

Relationship: Give to those ministries that you're involved in personally. If you represent your church, give money to those people or organizations that are getting your people out of the pew and into the community.

I just composed a letter to several in our church who we've been supporting in our community—some chaplains, others in parachurch organization. Here's that letter:

> We here at the church want to thank you for all your faithful service to our community over the years. You have been serving our Lord faithfully and have been fruitful. That's why we've been supporting you.

> We've recently made a philosophical change, and we'll be looking to support those ministries that get our people serving in the community. What we're asking of you is to train our people as you do your work. The more of our people that you take with you and train to do your ministry, the more fruitful we believe you'll be as you multiply yourself, and the more fruitful our people will be. The kingdom wins. To quote from Ephesians 4:10-13:
> "And He gave some as apostles, and some as prophets, and some as evangelists, and some as pastors and teachers, for the equipping of the saints for the work of service, to the building up of the body of Christ; until we all attain to the unity of the faith, and of the knowledge of the Son of God, to a mature man, to the measure of the stature which belongs to the fullness of Christ."
> We really do see the primary job of those we support as ministers in the community to be to train those in the body to do ministry. We'll do anything we can to get you into the many classes at church to share your ministry and to recruit folks to go with you. We're even glad to interview you in front of the whole congregation to connect you to those in the body. But fundamentally we believe local ministry is for everyone to be involved in, and our money will go to those getting our people involved and in touch with our community.
> Thanks,
> Jonathan

Accountability: Those we give to locally need to have systems of accountability. They're prone to the same sins as any of us. They need to be either directly accountable to a board of directors, the church, or a reliable and credible organization.

Transformation: As we discussed above, total transformation needs to be the goal—to take those who are stuck, and to see them transformed into those who help others get unstuck. Of course not everyone will be transformed—this is for certain. But if there's no plan for transformation, nobody will be transformed. This is also for certain.

Look at the plan. Look at the fruit. Are they simply enabling people to stay in their ruined state? Or is it giving hope and empowering them in the power of the Holy Spirit to be transformed into transformational agents?

Equity: To those whom much has been given—much is required. The wealthy in our society have a moral obligation to be involved with those who have not. When we step out of our own socio-economic places of comfort and into the lives of those who can not even afford health care—God shows up.

The gospel knows no bounds, but often in our churches we create artificial walls that get us stuck in our own social class. Breaking out of this transforms our own lives just as much as we can be used to help transform the lives of the needy all around us.

Chapter Sixteen

Throwing Candy or Taking the Good News?

Positions and tools of power have been given by God so that they might be used to empower others. And we must render account to God if we abuse or simply misuse this power.

When we were in greatest need, God gave us Jesus—not candy.

Many have seen the surreal photos of the fantastic mountains of Guilin in Southern China. Peaks that rise like great chess pieces tower over the surrounding rice fields and rivers. This most beautiful place in China happens to be one of the poorest regions in the country, and in the late 80s, as I traveled to the region, it was poverty like I hadn't seen anywhere else in my life.

Wanting to see the most scenic section of the Li Jiang (Li River), I signed up for a tour boat that would float down the river beneath these 500- to 1,000-foot monoliths. As much as I hate doing the "tourist thing," I couldn't resist the beauty of this region.

As we began the several-hour boat ride down the river, we entered regions inaccessible by road, and the poverty of the families living on the banks of the river increased with every mile we floated away from the small village where we had launched. The clothing the children wore was tattered, torn, and dirty. The children had no shoes. I hadn't seen children without shoes in China, and I'd been in the country for over five months. The children were thin and malnourished. My heart ached. Here we were—rich tourists on a boat of pleasure and of plenty. And though I got on board to see the natural beauty around me, instead I was faced with the great need of those who happened to have been born here.

The disparity was too much for many of the tourists aboard. We all felt guilty. But what could we do? Some had come prepared. In some tourist book, some of the passengers had read that they would come face to face with this poverty and so they were prepared to give.

Out came the bags of candy. They threw the candy upon the banks of the Li Jiang. Children yelled "Hallo," and raced along the shore over the rocks and sticks in their bare feet. For as far as they could, they followed the boat that rained candy upon their shores. After filling their pockets they would go back up stream to wait for the next boat. Yes, there they would wait for the next batch of generous rich people so willing to share their wealth.

So what is gained? Rich westerners with appeased consciences, and little poor children who now have to deal with rotten teeth and possible other health problems.

Will we Christians in the West continue to give in such a way that serves only to appease our consciences? In a way that serves to cripple individuals and churches?

Or will we learn to invest generously and wisely? Will we seek to make a real and lasting change for good? A difference for eternity?

> *Will we Christians in the West continue to give in such a way that serves only to appease our consciences? In a way that serves to cripple individuals and churches?*

Our resources can help advance the message of the good news, and they can empower the poor to live lives of dignity. But they will never do so simply because we share our resources generously with them. We must share our resources *wisely,* investing them so they'll produce much fruit.

> So he who had received five talents came and brought five other talents, saying, "Lord, you have given me five talents; look, I have gained five more talents besides them."
>
> His lord said to him, "Well done, good and faithful servant; you were faithful over a few things, I will make you ruler over many things. Enter into the joy of your lord." (Matthew 25:19-22)

GIVING WISELY?

Epilogue:

A Parting Parable: Ash or Treasure?

Written as a dramatic monologue for our relief weekend at church

> Now if any man builds on the foundation with gold, silver, and precious gems, or with wood, hay, and straw; each man's work will become evident; for the day will show it because it is to be revealed with fire, and the fire itself will test the quality of each man's work. If any man's work which he has built remains, he shall receive a reward. If any man's work is burned up, he will suffer loss; but he himself will be saved, yet so as through fire. (Paul the apostle)

Ahh, what a dream. Weird. Really wild. I awoke thinking, "Sheesh, where did that come from?" Maybe it was all this talk about Social Security reform. Obama's plan for retirement. The Democratic plan. The Republican plan. Yeah, that must be where it came from.

The dream was about an extremely bizarre "retirement plan" that had been implemented here in Oregon. And boy, did they have the most unusual and radical plan. At age 65, everybody *must* retire —like it or not—to a place called "Paradise Heights."

Now remember, this is a weird dream, so I'm not responsible for the content. This place was strange. But here were these two guys— a very wealthy Mr. Bill (as I remember his name), and a guy who didn't seem too rich, called Mr. Wally. Having been born on the same day, June 4, 1942, it was now time for both to retire. And they were nervous—for good reason. In just a few minutes it would "all" be determined for them by the authorities. And we're not talking bureaucrats in Washington. No politicians, red tape, or loopholes here.

You see, the value of their present estate would be calculated, and its worth would determine the worth of the place they'd have over yonder. The retirement place. Oh yeah, Paradise Heights.

But like I said, this place was weird. No bureaucracy and none of these "county appraisers" that come sneaking around with binoculars, trying to spy inside your home, like the ones I am used to. Nope. Here in my dream the folks that came out to test the real net worth of your estate—you'll never guess—crazy as dreams are—well, it was the "Oregon Fire Department," led by the fire chief himself.

Like I say, Bill and Wally were really nervous. Bill seemed extra jittery, but was trying his best to be confident. I saw them there in front of their homes as the fire truck pulled up. Bill's estate was enormous. An 8,000-square-foot home built of only the highest quality materials, and completely fireproof. He was prepared. He'd even installed a sprinkler system. If the already fireproof material somehow ignited, the system would spray the latest high-tech chemical that puts out *any* fire under *any* circumstance. Bill's place was gorgeous, immaculate, amazing—wow!

On the other hand, Wally's house next door looked pretty pathetic by comparison. A 1,200-square-foot home. Wooden. Simple. Nothing fancy, nothing really that modern. And nothing fireproof. It wasn't ugly, and actually was pretty tidy, but next to Bill's place—well, Bill thought it was the most pathetic thing he'd ever seen. He'd complained all his life about how Wally's house next door hurt the looks of his own place.

So there they stood. The fire chief whips out a little book of matches, lights one, and throws it onto Wally's lawn, which had turned brown from lack of water this summer. In all of a few seconds the lawn, the house—everything—goes up in a small poof of white smoke. Nothing's left.

Remarkably, somehow, Wally didn't seem that sad.

Bill tried not to laugh. Finally that place was gone, just as he'd always wished. And it took all of a couple seconds.

But wait, now it's Bill's turn. The fire chief lights the match and throws it down on Bill's well-watered, golf-course type lawn. Bill expects the match to go out the second it hits the lawn. It does not. It starts small and gains momentum as it approaches his gorgeous house. "What kind of fire is this?" But he knows, as I do, the house cannot burn, and the fire retardant will immediately get the fire out as soon as it gets within twenty feet of the house. He has prepared well and planned for this day of retirement.

Oops! The fire hits the house. And I cannot believe what I see. Ignition! Black inky smoke billowing thousands of feet into the air. Bill begins wailing as his estate sends up a cloud of fire and smoke not unlike the eruption of Mount St. Helens. The fire jumps from the house to the garage, which is twice

Ash. That's all that was left of both men's estates.

as big and twice as fancy as Wally's entire house. There his nice cars —and his 40-foot RV—just add to the columns of black. After a couple of hours of soaring flames and smoke, it's all over.

Ash. That's all that was left of both men's estates.

Wally walked over to the small pile of ash that had, just minutes before, been his house. It had been just a building to him, and he

EPILOGUE

knew that every memory he'd made in that home he would take with him to Paradise Heights. That simple thought was enough to make him grateful. But as he walked through the ash, he saw something sparkle. He bent over.

> But as he walked through the ash, he saw something sparkle. He bent over. It was a diamond.

It was a diamond. Not just one, but hundreds of tiny ones around the big one. He was puzzled. He'd had no diamonds in his home, where had they come from?

He began to reflect on the location of these diamonds. It was right where the dining room table had been. That table had been the center of their family—wow, the conversations about God that they'd had around that old beaten and scarred table. The missionary stories that had been told by the folks they'd supported overseas. The love and hope that was extended across that table to the countless guests whose lives had been shattered. As he picked up each diamond, a different memory would come to mind. He picked up a huge twenty-carat diamond and remembered how they as a family had talked about getting a new table to replace their old beaten one. But as soon as they brought up the discussion, his son had said, "Dad, let's just keep this one. It works fine. Give the three-hundred dollars you've saved to buy the new schoolbooks the kids need at the school our church started in Sudan."

Wally collected diamond after diamond from where that old beaten table had stood—each one evoking a memory and forming a tear of far greater worth than the diamond itself.

If Wally hadn't been so absorbed in thoughtful memories, he could have heard Bill wailing and crying like a spoiled child as he lay in his ashes lamenting his great and total loss.

Wally walked into the living room—or what had been the living room. Rubies. Rubies everywhere. A whole pile right in the spot—the memories came to him—where he used to wrestle his son nearly every day after work. A little over to the right a huge ruby was glistening right in the spot where there had been a huge coffee stain on the carpet. That was where their old drunken neighbor, Stan, who they'd taken in for a month, had spilled his coffee and left a huge stain. They'd talked about getting a new carpet, but again his son said, "No, Dad, give the eight hundred dollars to get Stan checked into the rehab program down at the rescue mission." Which they did. Stan ended up being like an uncle to their kids, and he finally was able to become a dad to his own.

Wally held up the ruby and watched it sparkle in the morning sunshine. "What a beautiful coffee stain!" he thought

Room after room—sapphires, pearls, onyx, topaz.

And then in the garage—even there. The biggest diamond of all right where their old '74 Ford Maverick had melted in the intense heat. Every time they'd saved up for a new car, they would hear of some need in Africa, or when they would think of making a car payment, some missionary would need support in order to leave for the field, and for some odd reason Wally and his family couldn't resist. He and his car were the laughing stock of the neighborhood, and Bill especially couldn't stand Wally's old piece of trash car.

But as Bill stood where his 2007 Humvee, his Jaguar XKR convertible, and his '57 Chevy had once been parked in all of what used to be their glory—he was inconsolable.

Wally, quite frankly, wouldn't miss that old Maverick even a little. He found all kinds of smaller precious stones around the huge

EPILOGUE

diamond that sat there. Conversations about Jesus came to his mind that he'd had with friends in that old trasher. People he'd stopped to help along the side of the road—talks—great talks with his kids. These were the things brought to mind by the precious stones.

Wait! Bill looked over with great hope. His fire-proof safe somehow had made it through the fire—he'd stored tons of cash and stock certificates in there—these would get him through retirement. He opened it eagerly and began kicking like a bratty child when he saw that all inside had been reduced to ash simply from the heat of the burning estate.

Wally took the several bags full of gems and precious jewels

> *"Last place on the right. The biggest most beautiful place we have. Well done, Wally. It's yours."*

and piled them into a wheelbarrow and then approached the gates of Paradise Heights. He handed over the gems to the gatekeeper and was given the keys. "Last place on the right. The biggest most beautiful place we have. *Well done, Wally. It's yours.*"

Bill sheepishly stepped up to the gates with a few small copper coins he'd found in the place where he used to write that check— somewhat begrudgingly—for his ten percent tithe to his church. He dropped them into the gatekeeper's hand.

"You'll be neighbors to Mr. Wally," the gatekeeper said.

"Oh, great! " Bill sarcastically replied. "But, I guess I'm used to it. Where are my keys?"

"Sir," came the reply from the gatekeeper, "Wally never locked his doors. You won't need keys. You've been in an exact replica— coffee stain and all—of his old place. Enjoy."

Strange place this was. Strange dream. Not sure exactly what it meant. And man, after a dream like that, I'm not sure at all we should be messing with Social Security.

E P I L O G U E